Garden Designers

John Brooks, page 105, lower left; Hugh Dargan & Associates, page 136; Ely & Associates, page 49, lower right; Environmental Creations, Inc., page 44; Greg Grisamore & Associates, pages 8, 9, 133, 134; John Herbst, Jr. & Associates, front cover, pages 46, upper left, lower right, 47, 48, 51, 52, upper left, 104, 139; Kate & Dick Maxey, pages 6, 56; Paradise Designs, Inc., page 11; Rathfon Landscape Architecture, pages 30, 130; Rogers Gardens, pages 21, 52, middle right; Sassafras Gardens, pages 7, 10, upper left; Nick Williams & Associates, page 19, lower right; Donna Wright, pages 58, 76, lower left, 90.

❦ A GARDENER'S GUIDE TO ❦
Planters, Containers & Raised Beds

Chuck Crandall & Barbara Crandall

Sterling Publishing Co., Inc.
New York

Designed by Judy Morgan

Library of Congress Cataloging-in-Publication Data

Crandall, Chuck.
   Planters, containers, and raised beds : a gardener's guide / Chuck
Crandall & Barbara Crandall.
      p.   cm.
   Includes bibliographical references and index.
   ISBN 0-8069-4242-8
   1. Container gardening.   2. Plant containers.   3. Raised bed
gardening.   I. Crandall, Barbara.   II. Title.
SB418.C735   1996
635′.048—dc20
                                                              96-6041
                                                              CIP

1 3 5 7 9 10 8 6 4 2

First paperback edition published in 1998 by
Sterling Publishing Company, Inc.
387 Park Avenue South, New York, N.Y. 10016
Originally published in hard cover as *Planters, Containers & Raised Beds*
© 1996 by Chuck Crandall and Barbara Crandall
Distributed in Canada by Sterling Publishing
℅ Canadian Manda Group, One Atlantic Avenue, Suite 105
Toronto, Ontario, Canada M6K 3E7
Distributed in Great Britain and Europe by Cassell PLC
Wellington House, 125 Strand, London WC2R 0BB, England
Distributed in Australia by Capricorn Link (Australia) Pty Ltd.
P.O. Box 6651, Baulkham Hills, Business Centre, NSW 2153, Australia
Manufactured in the United States of America
All rights reserved

Sterling ISBN 0-8069-4242-8 Trade
0-8069-4243-6 Paper

Page 6—
*Planters along the foundation provide convenient,
roomy repositories for tucking plants and trees
close in where they can be appreciated through the
season.*

Page 7—
*An antique garden cart brimming with color is a
charming and portable patio accent.*

Contents

Introduction

When the average person thinks of a garden, the image that usually comes to mind is a lushly planted plot of land devoted to annuals, perennials, and ornamentals or, perhaps, a vegetable garden or an orchard of fruit-bearing trees. But for millions of gardeners, the definition of what a garden is has been changing over the past two or three decades. These are the urbanites who reside in high-rises with no accessible garden space or in townhouses on tiny lots surrounded by paving. Their suburban counterparts often have space to garden, but few have the time to spare or the energy to invest in the preparation, planting, and maintenance of a conventional garden.

Does this mean that neither will be able to have a garden? Not at all. Instead it means they will probably have a garden that is different from the one their parents and grandparents may have tended. Theirs will be a *contained* garden of all sorts of plants, one that is aboveground and housed in pots, tubs, planters, or raised beds—one of the fastest-growing trends in gardening, the number-one American hobby.

Container gardening is an ancient skill. It can be traced back as far as the Pharaonic period of Egypt during which highly prized exotic plants from distant lands were grown in urns, protected from the punishing effects of the desert sun.

Today, growing plants in pots (and tubs, barrels, and planters) has become *the* way to garden for tens of millions of apartment, condo, and co-op dwellers who have only a balcony, terrace or rooftop on which to exercise their green thumbs.

Seniors and physically challenged people embrace pot, planter, and raised bed gardening because it means no exhaustive digging, weeding, or bending. In fact, it can even be done sitting down.

Finally, many who have the yard space and energy for a traditional garden prefer the advantages of container gardening over the conventional plot method. Among these benefits are the ability to tailor the soil mix to a particular plant's tastes, the elimination of strenuous shovel work to get the ground prepared each spring, and the convenience of having mini-gardens close to the house, where they can be tended easily and better appreciated.

Even though you may not totally convert your garden to containers and planters, we think you will find this method of growing everything from salad greens to fruit trees both fascinating and productive. Start with just a couple of pots of color to accent your entry and soon you'll be thinking of new ways to enjoy this easy, convenient way to garden.

—*Chuck Crandall & Barbara Crandall*

Built-In & Portable Planters

Windowbox and container gardens combine to create a stunning entry accent.

In recent years, planters designed as permanent features of outdoor spaces have become extremely popular in North America and Europe. New home designs often include built-in planters placed at convenient locations, such as flanking an entry, in the lee of a wall, or along the foundation or a perimeter wall.

Many homeowners are remodeling outdoor spaces to add planters, which are often designed to be integrated into privacy walls surrounding the property or placed along entry walls between neighboring homes to define property lines.

Materials for permanent planters are usually the same as those used to build the house, so they blend in with the original construction—brick, stone, wood, and concrete block (sometimes called cinder block). Concrete blocks are popular in construction projects because of their strength, versatility, uniformity of size, easy availability, and relatively low cost when compared with other materials. Often, concrete blocks are used to construct the basic planter or planter wall, then a veneer or facing of more attractive materials is applied to cover them. This may be bricks (half or whole), tiles, stone, or stucco which is then color-coated to match the exterior finish of the home.

If the house is a frame structure, some kind of wood is used to build the planter, thereby visually "wedding" the planter to the residence. Woods that are naturally rot-resistant are usually chosen—cedar, cypress, teak, mahogany, oak, or redwood—but other woods that are consid-

*P*lanters provide a contained space to grow virtually anything that can be planted in the garden—trees, shrubs, climbers, berries, vegetables, and flowers. The advantage planters offer is that they allow gardeners to grow greenery anywhere, and not merely where there happens to be open ground in the landscape.

Like containers, which are explored in the following chapter, planters can be filled with custom soil mixes and placed in just the right exposure for growing a wide variety of plants, particularly those with special needs, such as half shade/half sun days.

(**Page 8**) *Planters can be built into sloping terrain.*

(**Previous page**) *Built-in planters create sites for handsome mini-gardens.*

A low (2' high) planter is used to divide a driveway and an entry walk with an explosion of color.

Made of stuccoed block with brick trim, this handsome planter is a focal point in this backyard.

erably cheaper may be used after they have been treated with a preservative to retard rot and discourage borer insects. These include Douglas fir, which is structurally stronger than redwood, and pine, usually from the southern United States. Both of these, when treated with a preservative, will last for many years.

Another type of wood that is often used to construct planters is exterior-grade plywood, which is usually more economical to use than dimension lumber and takes a finish beautifully.

DESIGNS FOR PERMANENT PLANTERS

Built-in planters that will become a permanent part of the home landscape should be designed to meld architec-

turally with one's residence so they appear to be part of the original design. For example, a single-story brick ranch house calls for a low-level planter made or veneered with bricks that match those used on the facade of the house. Stone or other material would be jarring visually and make the planter appear to be just what it is, a retrofit.

For a contemporary two-storey stucco house, planters might be stuccoed "boxes" of varying heights, the tallest at the back corners and stepping down toward the middle or front (see photo).

With any additions to original construction, there is the danger of overdoing it, creating a massive structure that is out of scale with the existing architecture. It is always advisable to first lay out the project to scale on graph paper, along with existing structures. This will give a clear image of how the finished job will integrate.

Raised bed garden filled with seasonal color adds charm to this Victorian home.

Walls that don't retain soil are routinely erected by homeowners who have only a modest amount of masonry skill. These may be mortared stone or unmortared dry-laid stone, brick, and walls made of concrete block that are usually stuccoed or finished with brick or stone. Walls are not difficult to build and permits are not always required by local building departments, unless a variance is needed because the placement or height of the wall is in conflict with an existing ordinance. (See "Staying Legal" in the Appendix.)

Two important requirements should be borne in mind when building mortared walls: 1) Each course must be kept level so the finished wall will be "true;" 2) Footings of the proper depth and width, strengthened with reinforc-

Another reality check for those who may be a bit intimidated by the scope and scale of a proposed project is to consult a landscape architect or landscape contractor who can offer valuable advice on the design and construction plan. Many of these professionals will consult for an hourly fee that averages around $50 (see Appendix).

One of the most popular designs for planters is the combination planter and privacy/security wall that creates a front courtyard (see photo). With ambitious projects such as this, the opportunity to add planters on both sides of the wall, or a wall-hung water feature, is hard to resist. Plumbing for delivering water to the fountain and electrical conduit for lighting and powering a submersible pump for the water feature can easily be installed as the wall is built.

Planters that incorporate a retaining wall as the back of the planter require careful planning and design. They must be constructed so they can withstand the stresses brought to bear against them by tons of often unstable soil. Low retaining walls (3' and under) are not usually that difficult to engineer and often don't require a permit and inspection. Walls over 3' are not projects the average homeowner with only basic construction expertise should undertake. Most city or county building departments in the United States do require a permit and plan approval before retainers over 3' can be erected. This is one project that is best farmed out to a landscape architect, civil engineer or contractor who has had some experience designing and building these complex elements.

Entry planter made of stuccoed block with tile trim provides a cheerful welcome.

ing rods (rebars), are vital to the stability of walls over 3' tall.

Many permanent planters, whether free-standing or integrated into a wall, have no base but are open to the native soil. This enables roots to eventually reach below grade to develop normally and promotes efficient drainage.

Planters that are built on a slab or with a solid base must have drainage holes drilled in the bottom, or weep holes need to be installed by drilling holes into the bottom of the front or back wall of the planter (see illustration).

Free water that collects at the base of retaining walls must be drained or it will undermine the wall. The easiest method of handling this is to lay down sections of French drain pipe, which has holes every 5"–6". Water that is collected in the pipe through these holes is then carried away from the wall and dispersed to other parts of the yard (see illustration).

FOOTING POURED FOLLOWING THE 3–4–5 RULE

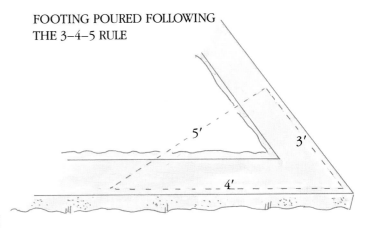

Precise 90° angled corners for planter boxes are easy to achieve by applying the "3-4-5 rule," which is explained in the text below.

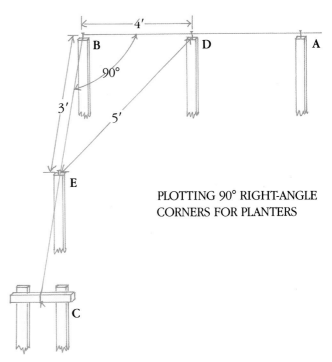

PLOTTING 90° RIGHT-ANGLE CORNERS FOR PLANTERS

In the construction of mortared planter walls (or any wall, for that matter), straight lines are established by measuring and driving stakes at precise points.

This illustration demonstrates the positioning of stakes and batterboards to correctly plot a right-angle corner. You'll need two measuring tapes, nails, a hammer, twine, and stakes.

Concrete blocks were used to build the basic wall on this terraced site; then a stone veneer was applied.

BUILDING MORTARED PLANTERS

Once a suitable design for a planter is in hand and any required permits have been obtained, preparation for construction may begin. Generally, the first step is to mark the boundaries of the planter using cord stretched between batterboards or stakes.

To plot an accurate right-angle corner for planters that are designed with precise 90° angles, the correct method is to employ what is called the "3-4-5 rule" (see illustration). This technique involves starting with the rear dimension. First, a straight line for the back of the planter is established. Next, an accurate right-angle corner for the planter is plotted. This is done by establishing the second line (known as B-C) perpendicular to the A-B line and tying off the twine to the crosspiece at a batterboard at point C.

On the A-B line, install a stake exactly 4' on center from

BUILDING PLANTER WALLS

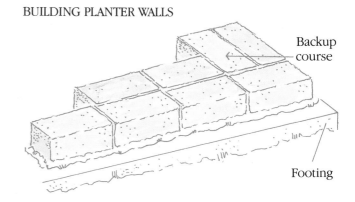

Backup course

Footing

Footings for planter walls are designed twice as wide as they are deep for maximum stability.

Another example of conquering a slope with basic walls of block that are dressed in stone.

Built-In & Portable Planters
15

stake B. This new stake becomes point D. Drive a nail halfway down in the top center of stakes D and B. For the next step, two steel tape measures are required. Hook the end of the first one over the nailhead in stake B and the second one over the nailhead in stake D. While holding the ends in place on the nailheads, have someone extend both tapes until the 3' mark on the tape hooked on stake B crosses the 5' mark on the tape attached to stake D. Drive a new stake in the ground at this point, which becomes stake E and insert a nail half way into the center top of this stake. Slide the cord attached to the batterboard crosspiece until it is precisely over the nail in stake E. Once this is done, a precise 90° angle has been achieved.

A straight wall or fence begins with the driving of the first stake into the ground, then follows the established procedure outlined in the text.

Mortared stone planters with walls around three feet high are sturdy and long-lasting. A cap of flat stone creates comfortable bench seating.

As a general rule, footings for walls are twice as wide as the width of the wall and one to two times as deep as the wall width. For example, a wall that is 8″ wide would have a footing 16″ wide and 8″–16″ deep.

In areas of ground freezes, the footing is poured into the trench over a layer of gravel from 4″–6″ deep, although depth requirements vary from city to city. In Sunbelt states, the gravel bed is often omitted. In both cases, the earth at the bottom of the footing trench should be compacted and level.

Once these calculations have been made, the trench is dug to the proper depth and width and reinforcing bars, popularly called rebars, are set in place. Then it is time to pour some "mud."

If the project is extensive, the task will go much faster if a concrete mixer is bought or rented. Hand-mixing dozens of wheelbarrows of concrete is a tedious, time-consuming chore. Both gas and electric-powered mixers equipped with a tow hitch are available from equipment rental outlets and many lumber yards. Larger firms carry sizes ranging from the small-capacity models that will mix five-gallon-pails of concrete at a time to contractor types that can handle four cubic feet.

You may, of course, mix your own concrete, but it is much simpler to buy dry ready mix, which is universally available in 60-lb. bags. These are offered in gravel-mix and sand-mix. Use gravel-mix for foundations for planters and retaining walls.

When mixing concrete, follow the instructions printed

A mason's line level on tightly stretched twine should be used to ensure that fence or wall elements are level.

on the bags to achieve the correct consistency. Concrete should be neither too stiff nor too wet or it won't form properly. The goal is to mix the batch so it is workable but doesn't leach excess water when it is poured. It is always wise to add less water than recommended and to check the consistency before adding more. Concrete is completely mixed when all the ingredients are coated and the overall color is uniform.

Fill the prepared trench with concrete and level it off with a screed board. Allow the foundation to cure overnight, then begin construction of the planter using bricks, blocks or stones. Use a mason's level to check each course. If cement blocks are used, insert rebars into the cells and fill these with concrete for additional strength.

For blocks and other materials that require cutting, use a silicone-carbide abrasive blade in a circular saw.

Those who have always wanted a stone planter or courtyard wall but have been put off by the cost and difficulties of working with natural stone may find the new generation of manufactured stone is the answer. It is made to resemble the real thing closely, but is only a fraction of its weight.

A number of manufacturers make precast stone with a mixture of tinted concrete and a variety of lightweight aggregates. Sizes and shapes vary to provide greater design flexibility and the back of the stone is flat to ensure a more secure mortar bond.

Manufactured stone is installed just like real stone. It can be mortared to any unpainted and unsealed surface, including concrete and brick and is ideal as a finishing material for concrete block walls.

Prices and types vary from source to source. Many larger building supply outlets stock manufactured stone, but usually only one or two types—river rock and flagstone, for example. You may be able to get the exact stone you want special-ordered for you.

When constructing a planter with a retaining wall in front of a slope of unstable soil, the placement of the retainer should be 6″–12″ in front of the slope. Fill the space between the wall and the slope with soil from another area. This obviates having to cut into the slope to accommodate the wall and possibly undermining it further.

The easiest retainer to build is the cantilevered type set on a wide footing that is four to five times the width of the wall. A gravel bed several inches deep and thick is established behind the wall before fill soil is added. For drain-

Construction supply outlets stock many sizes and shapes of concrete block elements. Shown here is a basic footing for a wall with rebars in place.

Cells of concrete block are generally filled with mortar to strengthen the wall. As mortar begins to set up, rebars may be inserted.

A concrete planter wall is kept true and level by the mason's line, which is adjusted upward for each new course of block.

Planter or retaining wall may be finished with a veneer of stone, tile, etc. Here, a scratch coat is applied in preparation for a stucco finish.

Planters, Containers & Raised Beds

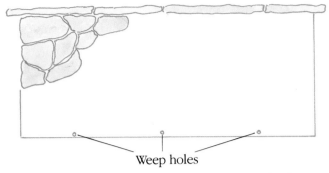

Weep holes

This block wall, veneered with stone, has had weep holes bored near the base.

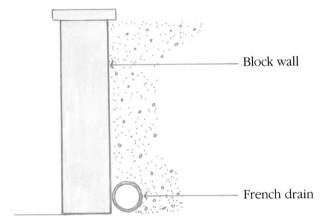

Block wall

French drain

Sideview of a wall with a French drain at its base.

age, either position French drains at the back base of the wall, as shown in the drawing, or bore weep holes in the front.

Rebars should be used in the footing and in the masonry units to bond the wall and the footing. The footing trench should be 1' deep, but may have to be deeper in areas of ground freeze since the bottom of the trench in these locales must be below the frostline.

BUILDING UNMORTARED STONE PLANTERS

In the right location, a stone planter or wall made of native rock is a handsome addition to the residential landscape. Most stonework is mortared for stability and permanence, but low stone walls have been dry-laid for centuries by landowners to mark boundaries.

Stone planters are more difficult to erect than those

Rubble stone retaining walls, mortared only with loam, are stable if kept three feet or under in height.

A correctly built dry-laid stone retaining wall planter. Note backward slant construction (battered construction technique).

BUILDING A DRY-LAID STONE PLANTER

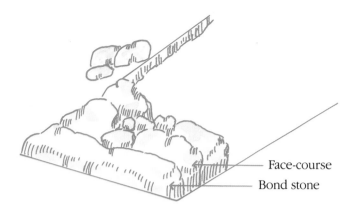

Face-course
Bond stone

Drawing shows the first course of stone for the dry-laid stone wall planter described below.

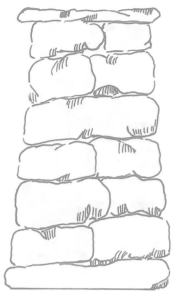

A properly constructed dry-laid stone wall.

made of brick or concrete block. Not only is the weight of the units greater, their shape makes secure positioning a genuine challenge.

A dry-laid stone planter is held together by the weight of the stones above pressing down on the stones below. For a dry-laid wall to be stable, the proper assembly technique is crucial.

First, dig a trench 6″–8″ deep and just wide enough to accommodate the width of the planter walls. Start with a bond stone (see drawing), which is a stone that spans the width of the wall. Next, start setting face course stones on each side of the wall. Trial the stones for fit, putting them in place then turning them until each fits snugly. There will always be gaps between stones and these should be filled with stone rubble that is tamped securely in place.

Greatest stability is achieved in a dry-laid wall if it is battered, a construction term that means "sloping inward." Both faces of the wall should batter about 1″ for each foot of rise.

Once a course is complete, begin another, following the same technique and making certain none of the vertical joints line up with the one below.

When the walls are completed, use the flattest, longest stones for the cap. If you live in an area of winter freezes, it is a good idea to mortar the cap stones in place, to block access to water seeping down into the interior of the walls where it can freeze and heave the stones out of place.

BUILDING WINDOW AND PORCH BOXES

Boxes for window sills, porches, decks, and patios are easy to find at garden centers and even through direct mail sources, but the prices are usually much higher than the cost of buying the materials and making them yourself.

Constructing boxes in squares and rectangles requires no advanced woodworking skill. If the boxes are assembled with butt joints rather than mitered edges, one simply cuts the lumber to size and assembles the boxes with stainless steel, hot-dipped galvanized or aluminum alloy fasteners and waterproof adhesive at the joints. Use screws in the assembly of major components for greater strength. Rustproof brads and nails may be used for affixing trim pieces.

If the cost and weight of materials are important considerations, and you have access to a table saw, use exterior grade plywood or other sheet goods (described in the section on lumber) to make boxes. Large (4×8′) sheets of plywood are difficult to cut accurately with a hand saw. Some lumber yards will rip plywood sheets to size for a nominal charge. This service is well worth the extra cost.

Dimension lumber is more convenient to work with since it is necessary only to cut boards to the desired

Wall-hung planter boxes made of rot-resistant wood bring garden color to the windows. This example blends well with the house style.

Built-In & Portable Planters

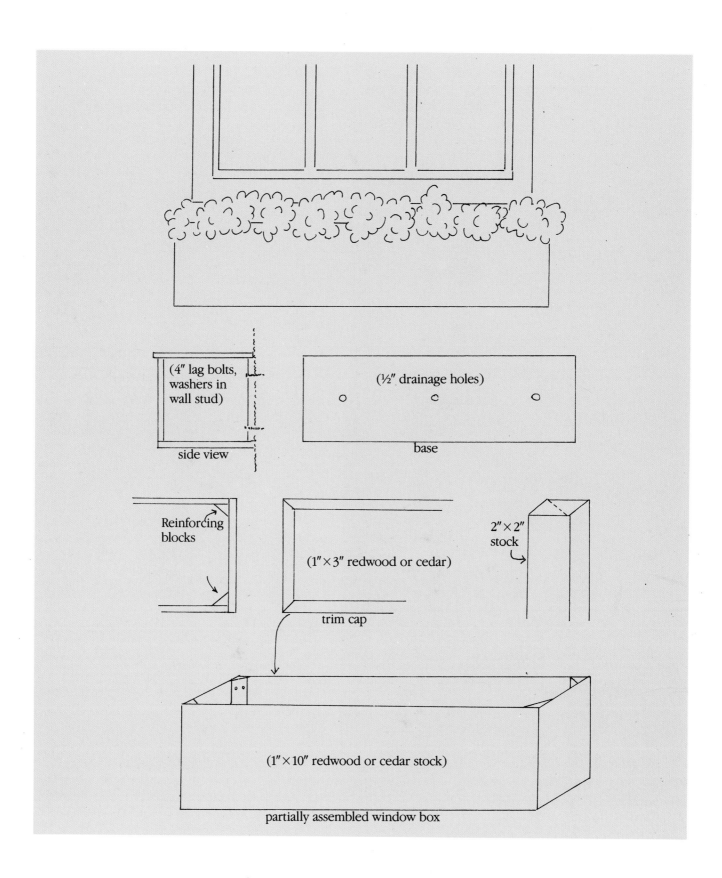

(4″ lag bolts, washers in wall stud)

side view

(½″ drainage holes)

base

Reinforcing blocks

(1″×3″ redwood or cedar)

trim cap

2″×2″ stock

(1″×10″ redwood or cedar stock)

partially assembled window box

A colorful welcome is offered guests at this home featuring a windowbox and wheelbarrow bursting with bloom.

length. You can make clean miter cuts on it, unlike plywood which is too thin.

Boxes may be finished in a number of ways. First, if they will be planted in, instead of serving merely as a decorative holder for a container, some provision should be made to protect the interior from premature deterioration from moisture. This can be done by using a coating of asphalt-based sealer, stapling heavy mil (6.–10.) landscape plastic or butyl rubber pond fabric to the interior and bottom, or sealing the wood and coating the inside with a least two topcoats of a quality enamel.

To prevent rot and avoid staining the surfaces where the boxes are placed, attach cleats to the base of the boxes to raise them a few inches off the ground. Drill a number of ½″ drainage holes in the bottom to evacuate excess water.

Stains and other finishes will protect wood from UV and moisture damage and enhance the appearance of boxes, especially if they are tinted to match or blend in with the house trim or color. Finishes are described later in this chapter.

Window boxes that are installed on high-rise sills and planters that are perched on ledges above walkways must be firmly attached to avoid potentially tragic accidents. Window boxes may be secured with metal straps and anchored into the framework of the structure by long screws. Also, rustproof screws may be driven through the bottom of the box and into the sill. If boxes are hung below the sill, lag bolts that have been inserted through the sides or back of the box and into framing studs are recommended. Also, expansion shields may be used to attach boxes to brick, stone, and stucco walls. These employ a lead shield that is driven into a hole drilled into the wall's

Containers and windowboxes in a riot of color enhance the front of this cottage. Plants are changed with the seasons.

surface. When a lag bolt is screwed into the shield, it expands and holds the bolt securely in place.

Planter boxes can be secured by attaching L-braces to their bases or legs and affixing these to trim or other structural elements.

Selecting Wood for Boxes and Planters

Solid-sawn dimension lumber, the trade description for conventional lumber carried in building supply outlets, comes from both deciduous hardwood trees and evergreen (cone-bearing) softwood trees. These two terms have no relevance to the real hardness or softness of the wood; it is merely how the trees are classified botanically.

Wood for boxes and planters is generally chosen for durability and resistance to borer insects and rot from

exposure to and contact with moisture. These are usually softwoods such as cedar, cypress, and redwood, all of which have a natural resistance to decay from moisture and wood-destroying fungi and insects. Hardwoods such as mahogany, oak, and teak also resist moisture damage but are less commonly used because of their higher price.

Although these long-lasting woods are preferred for contained gardens, less stable woods such as pine, hemlock, hemfir and spruce may be used if they are 1) sealed or coated with a preservative compound, 2) sealed and stained or painted with two topcoats, or 3) stained and given a water-repellent finish. These woods should not be buried or placed in direct contact with the ground unless they have been treated at the mill with a preservative, since this would hasten their deterioration from decay.

With the introduction of grading systems that rate the quality and stability of woods, lumber shopping has become somewhat less frustrating for the novice woodworker. These ratings reveal the moisture content, source, grain pattern, and other characteristics. This information is stamped on the ends of milled lumber from the majority of suppliers.

Most lumber millers in the U.S. use a grading system that follows the guidelines established by the American Lumber Standard Committee. Using this system, lumber is graded (and priced) by the part of the tree from which it is taken, how the grain runs (vertically or flat), how it is finished (rough sawn or surfaced, which means planed smooth), and how it is dried. But some woods (pine, for

A handsome deck designed to accommodate built-in planters. Planters are open on the bottom for efficient drainage.

A rustic windowbox is used in an unconventional spot—and entry wall—with charming results. The homemade bench serves as a quaint plant stand.

example) have their own separate rating system and some producers have developed their own standards. The best course, when in doubt, is to ask at the local lumberyard for an explanation of the ratings used for the lumber they stock.

Dimension lumber comes from either heartwood or sapwood. Heartwood, as the term implies, is from the center, or heart, of the tree. It has a tight grain that naturally resists rot, fungi, and borers and is the costliest lumber from a tree.

Sapwood grows between the heartwood and the bark. It contains the growth cells and carries food and water throughout the tree. Because of its high porosity, it is more susceptible to decay, but this characteristic also helps it absorb preservatives efficiently, as well as sealers, stains, and paints.

When lumber is milled and the bark removed, the grain of the wood can be seen. It may have a vertical grain, which runs the length of the board (the most desirable from the standpoint of stability), or a flat grain. Flat grain lumber is cheaper since it is more apt to warp, but if it is dried and stored properly, this propensity is curbed.

Each mechanical step in the production of finished lumber adds to its cost in the marketplace. Surfacing, or planing, is one of these steps. Lumber rated "rough" means that the surfaces have not been planed smooth. "Surfaced" means the stock has been smoothed and contains few knotholes or other defects. Surfaced four sides is the most desirable (and costliest) rating.

Drying is another factor in the cost equation. All lumber contains moisture. It is the presence of moisture in the wood fibers that affects its stability. The more moisture present, the more likely the lumber is to warp. Warped lumber is nearly impossible to work with.

Most lumber mills aim for a 17% or less moisture content. This is achieved by two methods of drying: stacking the lumber in a protected environment and allowing it to season (air dry) for several weeks, or quick-drying it in a kiln. The latter process produces the most stable lumber. Seasoned wood is given one of three grades: S-DRY, MC 15 (both air dried, which reduces the moisture content to between 12% and 20%) and KD (kiln dried), which reduces the moisture to 6% and 8% and is the more desirable and expensive grade.

Simple planters such as this are easy to construct using 6 × 6" timbers or railroad ties and make attractive yard accents.

A mix of annuals, perennials, and cascading plants means there is always something colorful in this windowbox.

Finally, the cosmetic appearance of lumber is also rated. Lumber with few defects is designated "clear" or "select." If some flaws are visible, the rating drops to "common." Pine that has no or only one or two minor defects is called "clear" or "appearance," and dubbed "common" if some knots are present.

Redwood, like pine, has its own grading nomenclature. The top grade is "clear all heartwood," which means that one surface is free of any defects and the other side can have only one or two pin knots. "Clear" may have a few small, tight knots or small checks. "Select heartwood" may have a few tight knots. "Construction heart," or "con heart," is the grade designated *garden grade*, indicating its suitability for outdoor projects. It usually has tight knots and some minor flaws.

"Select" may be mostly sapwood and is good for projects that will be above ground. "Construction common" is another all-purpose grade and may have several knots. "Merchantable" usually has large knots, some of which may be loose, as well as other defects, such as sap pockets and checks. This grade is often used for portions of projects that won't be visible.

Unless a project is going to be left unfinished or treated with a semi-transparent stain, there really is no need to spend the extra money for clear or select stock. So long as knots are tight and surface imperfections have been filled and sanded, lesser grades are just as suitable and cost considerably less.

So-called "manufactured" lumber is also worthy of consideration for projects that will not be stressed by excessive weight and are earmarked for opaque finishes. These include structural-glued lumber in three types: end-jointed, or finger-jointed; edge-glued; and face-glued. Structural-glued lumber involves using a number of techniques to glue together strips of the same species or mixed softwoods to create standard lengths of lumber. The end product is virtually as strong as conventional lumber and substantially less expensive.

In addition to solid-sawn dimension lumber and structural-glued stock, less expensive types such as exterior grade plywood panels and oriented strand board may be used for boxes and planters. Oriented strand board (OSB) is a cross-laminated panel composed of compressed wood strands layered at right angles and bonded together with a waterproof adhesive. It is considerably more stable than flakeboard, particle board or pressed board.

Only exterior grade plywood or OSB panels should be used for planters that will be kept in outdoor locations. Unlike interior grades, exterior plywood veneers and layers have been bonded with a waterproof adhesive, making panels highly stable in harsh weather and damp environments.

Plywood is commonly available in a variety of thicknesses ranging from ⅛″ to ¾″, although some outlets may carry sheets that are thicker and longer than the standards. While interior plywood may be cheaper, it is unsuitable for outdoor use, where it will be exposed to the elements. Moisture will eventually cause the veneer layers to separate. Exterior grade plywood is usually stamped with grade and rating indicating its suitability for outdoor exposure. Even so, the edges should be coated with a sealer to prevent moisture from seeping between layers.

Exterior plywood is rated by the American Plywood Association from A to C, with A the highest quality veneer. If the wood is to be finished with semi-transparent stains, Grade A will produce the most attractive results. Some producers have developed their own rating system that lists N as the premium grade.

Recommended fasteners include those made of stainless steel, hot-dipped or hot-tumbled galvanized steel, and aluminum alloy. Screws hold better than nails and make disassembly, if needed, easier. When using screws in plywood, always drill pilot holes to avoid splintering veneers.

Trim Tricks

Plain boxes may easily be dressed up with moldings that give the finished containers an expensive, professional look. Many lumber yards and wood craft shops stock moldings in a wide variety of profiles.

Use trim especially to cover and seal joints when constructing planters of dimension lumber, particularly those that will be planted in. Try a contrasting finish color for the decorative trim to add character to the planters and boxes you make or buy.

Vertical garden made of redwood boxes inserted into openings in framework. Boxes are removed for replanting or watering.

A simple box of cedar scrap makes an elegant state-ment when filled with caladiums and ferns.

WOOD PRESERVATIVES—WHAT THEY ARE AND WHAT THEY DO

Several wood types that don't have a natural resistance to rot from moisture and damage from burrowing insects can be treated with preservatives that protect them from these two major enemies of wood.

There are four preservatives that have commonly been used by lumber companies in the past, some of which are stringently restricted by the EPA for use because of their toxicity to the ecosystem: *Creosote,* a coal tar–based liquid that has a strong odor and a dark, oily appearance; *Penta-chlorophenol,* or penta, a chemical that can be combined with light petroleum oil, liquid petroleum gas, or solvents (called Cellon in the trade). Oil-borne penta has a slight odor and an oily surface appearance, which makes wood treated with it unsuitable for painting or staining. Wood treated with water-borne or solvent-borne penta produces an oil-free surface that takes a paint or stain finish; water-borne arsenical preservatives such as *Chromated Copper Arsenate* (CCA), which is the most popular preservative for treating solid-sawn dimension lumber and exterior grade plywood. Wolmanized wood is CCA-treated; and *Copper-8-quinolinolate,* which is dissolved in liquid petroleum gas or light hydrocarbon solvents that leave treated surfaces clean and free of solvent odor.

Most preservative-treated wood may be finished after it has cured for at least six months. The exceptions are creosote-treated stock and lumber containing oil-borne penta.

There are a number of precautions to take when using treated lumber containing the first three preservatives. Wear a dust mask or respirator when machining or hand-sanding these woods; keep such woods away from public drinking water sources; never burn scraps—dispose of them in the rubbish bin.

Creosote-treated woods are often used to create raised bed and retaining wall gardens. Before using such woods, make sure they have been treated with an effective sealer, such as urethane, epoxy, or shellac, which are rated accept-able sealers, to prevent preservatives from leaching into the soil. Also, food crops should not be grown where creosote-treated, penta-impregnated or arsenic-preserved woods are used, even if they have been sealed. Where food crops will be planted, copper-8-quinolinolate-treated woods are the best choice for planters and other con-tainers, in lieu of redwood, cedar and other naturally rot-resistant materials.

CCA-treated lumber has a pale green hue that eventually weathers to a light grey. It can be sealed and either stained or painted.

FINISHES FOR WOOD CONTAINERS, PLANTERS

Naturally rot-resistant woods such as redwood and cedar don't require a preservative or sealer, although portions of structures constructed with these woods, especially sap-wood portions, that contact the ground benefit from a sealer/preservative applied in two successive coats. Left unfinished, cedar and oak grey slightly with exposure to the elements and redwood ages to an overall driftwood grey. In areas of severe weather or long rainy seasons, such as the Pacific Northwest, a sealer coat renewed annually does prolong both the life and attractive appearance of these woods.

Decay-resistant woods may be stained or painted to match the color of one's home. Before finishing wood with a sealer, stain, or paint, its surface should be free of dirt, sap, and mildew and it should be thoroughly dry. Dirt is best removed with a strong detergent and a stiff-bristled brush. Mildew, which appears as splotchy black or light grey stains, can be neutralized and removed with a brush dipped in a solution of one part chlorine bleach to three parts warm water. Repeated treatments may be needed and

Planters were cleverly integrated into the bench supports on this small deck. They drain below onto the ground.

appropriate eye, skin, and clothing protection should be worn. There are also commercial mildewcides on the market that are equally effective.

Extractive staining may appear on the surface of some woods, particularly redwood, which should be removed before finishing. Staining occurs when colored chemical compounds (extractives) that are present in some woods work their way to the surface. This can happen when wood becomes damp or when it is coated with a latex (water-based) finish if the wood has not first been treated with a stain-killing sealer. Extractive stains usually can be removed by wiping down the affected areas with a solution of oxalic acid, which is available at paint and building supply outlets. The usual dilution ratio is four ounces of oxalic acid dissolved in a gallon of warm water. Flush the treated area with clean, warm water and allow it to dry before sealing or finishing.

Note that oxalic acid is toxic and can burn the skin. Use it only in a well-ventilated area and wear a respirator, gloves, eye protection, and appropriate protective clothing.

Stain Finishes

Wood stains are the ideal material for attractive, long-lasting and low-maintenance finishes. Stain provides good coverage and doesn't flake with age or the onslaught of seasonal weather extremes. Many brands contain a mildewcide, which is important in areas with long, severe rainy seasons. Like paint, stains are available in virtually any color, thanks to computer matching of swatch samples.

There are two types of stain: *semi-transparent*, which allows the wood grain to show through, and *solid-color*, which is opaque and covers the wood's color and grain but doesn't hide its textural characteristics. These highly pigmented finishes effectively mask patches and repairs and most knotholes. Incidentally, knots and sap pockets must be covered with shellac or other stain-killing sealers before finishing or bleed-through will occur.

Oil-based semi-transparent exterior stains, which reveal grain pattern and texture, are recommended by the American Plywood Association for finishing better grades of exterior plywood that will be exposed to weather.

Other woods weather well when finished with an exterior stain-blocking acrylic latex primer followed by one or two topcoats of exterior acrylic solid-color latex stain.

Paint Finishes

For both dimensional lumber and all APA rated plywood (except brushed plywood), the most satisfactory and long-lasting paint finish is achieved by applying at least one exterior primer coat and one topcoat of good quality exterior acrylic latex paint. For wood which tends to leach extractives, two primer coats are advised. Oil-based or oil-alkyd topcoats are not a suitable option since they are prone to premature cracking and flaking.

On the interior walls of planters and boxes that will be in contact with damp soil, apply several coats of sealer to prolong the life of the wood.

Windowboxes filled with flowering and foliage plants dress up this wall.

chapter 2

Containers—
Conventional &
Unconventional

In some cities, homeowners are permitted to install and maintain sidewalk planters such as these striking examples.

For those who reside in city apartments and town-houses with access to just a small terrace or balcony, containers provide the only opportunity to enjoy the pleasures of gardening outdoors, and every square inch of space is utilized.

But there are just as many people who have suitable ground space for a traditional garden who prefer to do most of their gardening in containers. They use them to direct "traffic" to a particular pathway, to fashion attractive barriers, to create sight screens where they want privacy and view blockers where they want to comouflage unsightly views. They find them valuable as a way to add instant color to a patio—color that can be changed with the seasons and can serve as handsome entry accents where paving precludes planting directly in the ground.

Additionally, containers enable gardeners in cold-winter climates to grow frost-tender plants that can, in advance of cold weather, be moved to a protected indoor location until the following spring. Finally, they allow the gardener to move plants that require specific exposures to take advantage of sun or shade through the growing season. By placing heavy containers on stands with casters made for the purpose (and which are stocked by many garden centers), plants that need to be shifted occasionally can easily and safely be trundled from one spot to another, provided the site is relatively level.

While nearly everyone has raised something as simple as a potted house plant or a trough of salad greens, it has only been in the last decade or so that shrubs, berries, and

Gardening in containers is unquestionably the most popular way to garden across the globe. There are gourmet cooks in France with windowsills full of potted herbs, bonsai masters in Japan who train centuries-old dwarf trees in ceramic trays, and rooftop gardeners in New York City who tend amazing assortments of containerized flowers, vines, and trees, creating a verdant retreat in a world of sterile concrete.

(Page 30) *Containers quickly dress up patios, terraces.*

(Previous page) *Hanging baskets are easy, colorful accents.*

For a quick, seasonal accent, cheery red poinsettias were planted in a hanging redwood basket.

A stairway was used to good effect as a staging area for a dazzling contained garden of spring bloomers.

both fruit and ornamental trees have been routinely grown in containers. One reason is that affordable pots of adequate size were not widely available until recent years; the other is a prevalent but erroneous belief that these kinds of plants only prosper in a conventional garden environment.

It is true that shrubs and trees that grow to mammoth proportions are not grown to maturity in containers, but there are dozens of shrubs that maintain a modest size and trees that are genetic or man-made dwarfs that may be maintained their entire life in containers of appropriate size. (See Chapter 4.) Containers for these may be generously proportioned plastic pots that hold 1½–2 cubic feet of soil or 24″–36″ half barrels or boxes.

Containers may be described as "conventional," which includes all those designed for planting in, and "uncon-

ventional," which are those that were made for other purposes, but which can be used as plant holders.

CONVENTIONAL CONTAINERS

Among the most popular of the traditional containers are the terra cotta (clay) pots that are available in a wide array of sizes from 2″ to behemoths 50″ or more in diameter. Plants seem to have an affinity for clay and usually prosper in pots made of this natural material, provided they are given the proper nutrition and adequate moisture levels.

Some of the most popular styles are the *standard flower pot,* which is usually twice as tall as it is wide at its mouth and has sides that slope inward toward the base. It has a thick rim that resists cracking if knocked over. There are also cylindrical versions without a rim or lip and with straight sides. These are commonly available in sizes from 6″ to 18″.

Azalea pots, which may also be called fern pots, are generally three-quarters as high as they are wide. These are often chosen for growing shallow-rooted plants that don't require the extra depth. Also, the scale between these shorter pots and plants like azaleas and ferns is often more visually appealing. These containers are made in sizes from 4″–18″.

MEXICAN POTS, OR OLLAS, are usually wider at the center and slope inward at the top and bottom. They are often adorned with designs etched into the wet clay before

The value of contained gardens may be seen here on this city townhouse terrace where the owners grow an array of shade-tolerant plants.

firing or decorations such as flowers and animals affixed around their sides. They are also thicker and heavier than most other clay pots of comparable size. Some are sun-dried and more porous and will deteriorate after a few seasons. Sizes range from 6″ to ones large enough to house a mature palm tree.

SPANISH POTS are more elegant in shape with their vase-like style. They have sides which slope outward toward the rim. They are made in sizes from 4″–24″.

VENETIAN, ITALIAN POTS resemble wide-mouth vases in configuration and have concentric, incuse rings from the base to the rim.

BULB PANS, BOWLS Pots for forcing bulbs, and bowls for dish gardens, are usually only a third to a half as high as they are wide. They are made in widths from 4″ to 24″, but larger sizes may be found in specialty garden or pottery shops.

Most standard types of clay containers are available in glazed finishes in a variety of colors. The advantage of glazing is that moisture, undissolved fertilizer salts (white encrustations) and minerals in tapwater can't leach through to the surface, creating an unattractive patina. But this can also create a problem if plants grown in glazed containers are routinely overfed and overwatered. With unglazed terra cotta, excess moisture containing some of the fertilizer residue is absorbed into the clay and passed

A diverse variety of containers, a few of which are shown here, are available at garden centers and from mail-order sources.

Plants in pots provide a ring of color around a garden sculpture. This arrangement also works well for encircling fountains.

through to the surface where it evaporates.

Those who find the staining of unglazed pots objectional may simply place them inside slightly larger glazed containers. Then, the translocation of excess moisture and salts through the clay (which is beneficial to the plant) is achieved, but the result is not visible. These stains, incidentally, can be removed from clay pots after the plant has been knocked out by using a stiff brush dipped in a solution of one part chlorine bleach to four parts hot water, then rinsing with clear water. Rubber gloves and old clothing are recommended for this procedure.

TROUGHS are usually decorated on their sides with decorative reliefs, cherubs, or other figures and designs. They are also made of concrete, metal, plastic, or fiberglass. Antique versions were carved from stone. They are of various sizes, but most fit comfortably on a typical window sill or wall.

PLASTIC, FIBERGLASS POTS, TUBS AND TROUGHS
Hard plastic and rigid fiberglass containers that mimic the shapes of classic pots and tubs have been around since the end of World War II as inexpensive alternatives to the pricier versions made of clay, stone, and metal. In recent years, flexible plastic containers in the full assortment of profiles and a broad range of sizes have gained wide acceptance among gardeners who prefer them because of their lighter weight. Others like the fact that they cost about a third of what a container of comparable size made of clay or ceramic sells for, which means an impressive pot garden can be put together without stressing one's budget.

Plastic and fiberglass pots come in a variety of colors, but the most popular hues are terra cotta red, which closely resembles clay, forest green, and white. These pots offer a number of benefits to the home gardener. Among these, as mentioned above, are their light weight, which makes them indispensible for rooftop and balcony gardens where weight is an important consideration. A 24″ clay pot or wooden tub filled with damp planting mix can easily weigh over 100 lbs. The same size plastic container will average less than half of this.

Another advantage these impermeable containers offer is that soil mixes in them stay moist two to three times longer than in those made of porous material. This is beneficial for plants that prosper in continuously evenly moist soil. It also reduces the volume and frequency of irrigation plants need. Plants grown in full summer sun in clay or wood may need irrigating every day, while those in plastic, fiberglass, or glazed containers can often go two or three days before needing additional water.

What is the downside to plastic pots? Because they preserve soil moisture longer and prevent fertilizer salts from leaching through their walls, care must be taken not to over-water or overfeed plants grown in them. Too much moisture or fertilizer is as deleterious as too little.

Probably the most serious drawback is that plastic, particularly in its rigid form, is made brittle by UV rays. Containers that have been exposed to the sun for just one season sometimes split easily when handled. Even so, their relatively low cost makes them a bargain.

Salad greens, herbs, and tomatoes are only a few of the edible plants that prosper in containers of the appropriate size.

No accessible ground for a garden? Planters and containers are the answer.

Plastic troughs are available in a variety of lengths and widths and are ideal planting liners for wooden or metal window boxes. They are also excellent for starting seeds and growing radishes, scallions, leaf lettuce, and shorter varieties of carrots.

For larger plants, such as shrubs and trees, for water gardens, and growing vegetables and other food crops, the favored container is one made of decay-resistant wood. Most of these boxes and tubs are crafted from redwood, cedar, oak or cypress, although other less stable woods may be used if they are sealed and stained or painted, or their interior is coated with a preservative compound such as asphaltum paint.

Hanging Gardens

As biblical history has recorded, hanging gardens have been around since King Nebuchadezzar of Babylonia exercised his green thumb and made his suspended gardens one of the Seven Wonders of the World 2,500 years ago. On a much smaller and more realistic scale, hanging gardens are created today using pots rigged for suspending and moss-lined wire baskets. The latter are fashioned by soaking sheets of sphagnum peat moss in warm water, squeezing out most of the moisture and pressing the moss against the inside framework of a welded wire basket. When the moss dries completely, it becomes a marvelous container for holding soil and plants. Also available are the new

Leaving barely enough room to walk, these bountiful baskets and containers create a feast for the senses on this sheltered patio.

This handsome three-tier hanging basket is filled with plants that thrive in a half-sun, half-shade exposure.

hemp and coconut fiber liners. (See Chapter 4 for suitable plants for hanging gardens.)

Other types of containers and hanging devices are available for suspended gardens at larger garden centers and from direct mail nurseries. Most popular among these is the plastic or clay pot with either a built-in or detachable saucer and pre-drilled holes for attaching hemp or wire hangers. There are also metal clips that can be used to hang small-to-medium-size clay pots on a wall or fence and another design that enables the pots to be suspended from a ceiling hook.

Formally clipped ivy topiaries contrast with the rustic informality of a wheelbarrow planter on this sun-drenched patio.

Planters, Containers & Raised Beds

UNCONVENTIONAL CONTAINERS

Unusual containers give a garden personality and add a note of interest. While some unconventional containers may lack the sleekness of imported pots, they often are just as functional and are available at a fraction of the cost. Here is a list (by no means a complete one) of novel containers that can be used to grow a wide range of plants.

SEWER PIPE, FLUE TILES Both clay and concrete sewer pipe and clay flue liners make ideal planters. They are open on both ends. If they are to be used on decks or patios, a catch basin or saucer of appropriate size will also be needed. Both are available at building supply outlets.

HOLLOWED-OUT LOGS, LOG ROUNDS These are handsome, natural planters. Logs can be suspended from overhead structures and log rounds may be attached to posts, fences and other verticals. These are easily made. Alternatively, ready-to-plant logs may be purchased at larger garden centers and craft shops.

BUSHEL AND OTHER BASKETS Good for one- or-two season gardens, the usefulness of these inexpensive containers can be prolonged by lining them with plastic (in which several drainage holes should be punched). Spray- or brush-painting baskets with an exterior enamel or applying a coat of opaque stain further enhances these rustic planters and helps extend their useful life.

FRUIT AND VEGETABLE CRATES AND BOXES Markets and produce stores are good sources of these free sturdy wooden crates which can be used a season or two to

Spring bulbs explode with color and aroma in these roomy half whiskey barrels, a popular informal container for growing virtually any plant.

A quarter whiskey barrel provides a whimsical framework for a garden of cascading color. Note the soil retainer boards on the lower half of the opening.

PILLOW PACKS Commercially prepared plastic packs in one- and two-cubic-foot sizes containing lightweight soil, perlite or vermiculite and a slow-release fertilizer are available at garden centers, but they can easily be made by filling large plastic trash bags with the same ingredients. Holes are made in the top for inserting seedling plants. After harvest, the soil mix may be added to the compost pile for recycling.

HALF BARRELS One of the most durable containers is the wine or whiskey barrel, usually made of rot-resistant oak. These barrels cut in half are ideal for housing dwarf

Sturdy, handsome planters of redwood house a stunning collection of spring-blooming bulbs, plants, and edible accents.

raise vegetable and flower crops. They are made "plantable" by stapling fiberglass screening ($2 for a 10′ roll) inside to keep soil from sifting through the openings between the slats. Give them a festive touch by spray-painting them vibrant colors.

PLASTIC TUBS, PAILS, AND BUCKETS For areas where they can be tucked out of sight, tubs that once held everything from drywall compound to bird seed, as well as other utilitarian containers, can have a new life instead of ending up in a landfill. With a few holes drilled in the bottom so excess water can escape, plastic tubs are useful for growing strawberries, herbs, lettuce, fingerling carrots, and seedling plants.

One- and two-cubic-foot bags filled with enriched soil and nutrients are available at garden centers for dig-free small-scale vegetable gardens.

Planters, Containers & Raised Beds

Attractive plantings can be in such uncommon containers as baskets and sphagnum.

Planters such as this lovely wrought-iron example are ideal for decks and terraces. Portable, they offer a color accent anywhere.

specimen trees, shrubs, grapes, berries, and vegetable gardens. They may even be used for fashioning a rustic water garden. Most building supply and garden centers stock them.

Often, the most visually appealing and inexpensive containers are stumbled across when haunting garage and tag sales or flea markets. Anything that has sides to hold soil and a bottom that can take drainage holes can be a potential candidate—an old, rusty wheelbarrow, an ancient watering can, or a Victorian doll bed.

The Importance of Good Drainage

Whenever containerized plants are watered, the excess moisture not absorbed by the soil mix works its way down to the base of the container. This surperfluous water must be evacuated to preserve the health of the plant's roots. Standing water in the bottom of a pot or tub blocks the entrance of oxygen into the soil mix, which is vital to the process of food-making *(photosynthesis)*, and eventually causes the delicate feeder roots to decay. Once this occurs, the plant is usually doomed.

While it is true that sharp drainage of excess water is desirable in most cases, the one exception is in semi-desert and desert climates, such as exist in southern California and the southwestern U.S., the Mediterranean region of Europe, the Middle East, and parts of Spain and Italy. It is beneficial for the soil mix in containers in these regions to retain a high volume of moisture for longer periods, to compensate for a plant's stepped-up transpiration caused by intense heat and dry, dessicating winds. This is achieved in four ways: 1) by using containers that are made of impermeable material, such as plastic, ceramic, fiberglass, or metal, as was mentioned earlier; 2) by reducing the number of drainage holes in the base, where this is an option; 3) by using a soil mix that has a greater proportion of water-retentive amendments, such as perlite and vermiculite, than is found in standard mixes; and 4) by using a drip irrigation system equipped with a timer that provides plants with a more or less continuous dribble of water around their roots.

Most containers made for growing plant material have one or more holes in their base. If there is no drainage opening, one or more should be made. Some pots have a break-out plug that can easily be punched out with a screwdriver and hammer. Holes in clay, concrete, and glazed ceramic containers may be made neatly with a power drill and masonry bit. Use a high-speed carbon steel bit for tin, lead and other metals.

Capturing free water that drains from containers is important—especially if one gardens on a terrace or rooftop, where the water would drip down on a neighbor's

Containers must have adequate drainage to prevent root rot. The most effective method of adding drain holes is with an electric drill and masonry bit.

To ensure efficient drainage and prevent pot bases from sitting in water that has drained in the catch basin, when it isn't convenient to collect it, use blocks of scrap wood, clay "feet" (see illustration), or bricks to raise containers an inch or two. This provides good air circulation around the container and inhibits a plant's tendency to send feeder roots out the drainage hole(s) to reach standing water.

To make sure that drainage holes are kept open and free of obstructions, some gardeners place a layer of rocks or shards of clay pots in the bottom of containers. Except for roof gardens, where combined pot weight might create a problem, this is a good practice, but a piece of coffee filter paper or rust-free fiberglass screen cut to size should first

Containers of color on a window ledge not only enhance the exterior but provide a pleasant vista for those inside.

balcony or terrace, or where it would fall on passersby in the street below. Also, if containers are kept on a deck or patio, drainage water can stain or damage the surfaces, especially wood.

The best solution is the one used for as long as containers have been in vogue—the catch basin, or saucer. A few minutes after irrigation, this water should be collected and disposed of. It should not be reused to irrigate plants because it may contain disease organisms and excess fertilizer residue flushed out of the soil mix.

For containers too heavy to lift to remove saucers, use a poultry baster to draw up the water and deposit it in a bucket for later disposal.

Exotic orchids are ideal pot plants for a bright window. They have only minimal roots and adapt readily to confinement in containers.

be positioned over the drainage openings. This prevents soil from escaping and blocks access to bugs, slugs, crickets, and other destructive chewing pests.

PROTECTING SURFACES As touched on earlier, moisture condensation and drainage water that contains dissolved fertilizers can permanently stain wood and paved surfaces under containers. Continuous contact between moist pots and untreated wood decking can eventually cause rot.

To protect surfaces on which contained gardens are maintained, use glazed saucers under pots. Natural terra cotta may be made somewhat waterproof by applying two or three coats of a clay sealer, available at many paint stores and garden outlets. Pots that leach moisture also may be placed inside containers made of ceramic or other nonporous material.

With planters that are allowed to drain onto paving and decking, to prevent permanent staining, wipe up standing water and clean areas under containers once a month with a 50–50 mix of chlorine bleach and warm water. To a great extent, this will also prevent mold and mildew. It's a good idea to shift containers and tubs periodically so they are not sitting in the same spot for long periods.

Finally, keep in mind that hard plastic containers are quickly aged by UV rays. If possible, keep these in shaded locations or spots that receive only morning sun. Also, darker colors absorb solar rays and the build-up of heat inside pots may stress roots. This can be avoided by restricting darkly tinted containers to shady nooks or by double-potting—placing them inside larger tubs with damp sphagnum moss or newspapers between them to serve as insulation.

3

Designing & Building Raised Beds

A simple planter created by sinking rot-resistant timber sections on end and filling the space with improved soil. Individual timbers were connected with rebars held in place with construction staples.

One of the most useful elements in the landscape is the raised bed garden which, like planters, may be tailored in size and shape to fit a particular location.

Raised beds are commonly used to accomplish a number of goals in landscape design. When they are placed opposite each other at an entry, they direct "traffic" to the front door and, when planted attractively, help create a favorable first impression—what realtors call "curb appeal."

For those with physical handicaps that limit or preclude bending, raised beds are very appealing, because they can be built high enough to provide easy access for planting and weeding without excessive bending or from a sitting position on the cap board or from a wheelchair.

They are truly useful in sites where the native soil is so hard, rocky, clayey or saturated by a high water table that gardening in it is difficult to impossible. When filled with improved loam, raised beds provide ideal conditions for growing everything from flowers for cutting gardens to specimen trees and prize-winning vegetables to succulent berries.

(Page 44) Stone planter is a handsome entry accent.

(Previous page) Raised bed planters fit just about anywhere in the garden.

In areas where the summer growing season is brief, raised beds enable one to get an earlier start. Because the soil is raised above grade, it absorbs solar heat more quickly and drains more efficiently than does native soil so seeds are not subject to decay from contact with cold, mucky earth. Seedlings started indoors adapt much faster in warm soil and consequently mature sooner.

In home environments where rambunctious pets and children tend to trample everything in sight, raised beds lift the garden out of danger. The walls of beds also block access to foraging roots of adjacent trees, shrubs, and lawn grasses that compete with other plants for moisture and nutrients. They also help contain the roots of plants that

This attractively designed and built terraced/ retaining wall garden was once a useless, steep backyard slope. Now, it is a landscape asset where cut flowers and vegetables are grown.

A double (stacked) raised bed planter, similar to the one on the preceding page, creates a stunning "hill garden" with conifers, Japanese maples, bulbs, annuals, and perennials.

tend to "run" and become invasive, such as bramble berries and some bamboos.

One particular area in the landscape where raised beds are indispensable is the steep rear yard slope that is so precipitous it is inaccessible for gardening. By terracing with raised beds and footpaths, these acclivities can be transformed into handsome assets. Because these structures retain tons of earth and require anchoring posts driven deeply into the ground, this project should be left to professionals. While it may seem a costly undertaking, one must weigh this against the benefit of enhancing the home environment by creating an attractive feature that is visually appealing and contributes substantially to both the usefulness and value of one's property.

RAISED BEDS FOR CROP PLANTS

For the reasons stated earlier, and for the sheer convenience of it, many gardeners throughout the world grow all or most of their vegetables, fruit, berries, and herbs in raised beds, while another large percentage grow their produce in planters and containers.

Roots of crop plants grown in raised beds extend deeper in their quest for moisture and a well-developed root system means healthier, more productive plants. It is also possible to extend the growing season, since it is easy to create temporary cold frames in raised beds. This is done by using clear plastic over them that is either stapled to stakes driven in at the corners or draped over flexible PVC pipe bent over the beds in the shape of an inverted U. The ends of the pipe are inserted in PVC pipe of a slightly

Conquering an inaccessible slope, the designer cut away earth to create terraced pads on which were constructed timber planters for growing a large vegetable garden in a concentrated space.

Planters, Containers & Raised Beds

A raised bed vegetable garden at a senior center was designed to be used by wheelchair-bound gardeners.

between raised beds and any barriers, such as fences or walls of 36″, although 40″ would be better.

Height of raised beds is also an important consideration. If you want to create seating-height beds, where you can sit on the cap and plant, harvest or weed, 18″–20″ is the ideal height to minimize leg and back stress. The cap should be a minimum of 6″ wide for seating comfort.

To make the planting area accessible without strain, bed height for wheelchair-access gardens should be 28″–30″. This positions the gardener at mid-chest level to the planting surface and enables him or her to reach across the bed without bending.

larger diameter that is sunk into the corners of the beds. In addition to shielding plantings from early frosts and biting winds, this technique creates a greenhouse effect—a microclimate where the environment is moist and warm. If the weather warms and the temperature or moisture level under the plastic becomes too great, the cover can quickly be rolled back or removed.

Where pests such as leafminers, cabbage worms, and other destructive insects are prevalent, floating spun row cover may be draped over these PVC frames to deny access to winged adults that lay their eggs on crop plants. This lightweight fabric admits sun, moisture, and air, but blocks access to flying insects. Many large garden centers stock it, or it may be obtained from mail order nurseries.

To maximize crop production, place raised beds where they will receive five or six hours of direct sunlight each day and lay them out north to south so that plants don't shade each other as they grow.

How much space to allocate between and around raised planters depends on who will be using them. For general access, 24″–30″ is adequate. This is enough space for a wheelbarrow to negotiate. A wheelbarrow is indispensable when bringing in fresh soil mixes and amendments and for general maintenance of these elevated gardens.

If the beds will be used by physically challenged or elderly gardeners confined to a wheelchair, provide enough room to accommodate the chair comfortably and to rotate it with ease. This requires a minimum distance

An attractive solution for taming a precipitous slope, these terraces of landscape timbers create visual interest and reclaim more backyard space for family use.

Many herbs have shallow roots, making them ideal plants for pot and planter culture. Here, nearly a dozen herbs reside together in harmony.

Beds may be as long as one wishes to make them, but their width should not exceed four feet. Wider beds make it difficult to reach the center of the planting area easily from the sides.

When planning raised bed gardens, consider the type of flooring that will be needed. For wheelchair access and maneuverability, a firm, level surface constructed of brick, concrete, flagstone, or compacted decomposed granite is best. For general use, a layer of gravel 3″–4″ deep over perforated plastic or landscape fabric (for improved drainage and to eliminate weeds) is suitable and inexpensive.

Raised beds are generally designed as four-sided planters open on the bottom to the ground. Roots of plants grown in them may extend into the native soil over which they are built. Some gardeners add a layer of gravel in the bottom of the beds to enhance drainage. This does not impede the expansion of roots into the ground. Other gardeners churn up the earth under beds and mix in amendments such as peat moss, manures, or fertile topsoil to encourage deeper root penetration. This extra step is unnecessary, since the roots of most crop plants confine themselves to the depth of mixes used in raised beds, especially if they are a minimum of 18″ deep. The exceptions are tomatoes and corn, whose roots can descend six feet or more, and some berry and fruit species whose roots may grow even deeper.

If gophers, moles, and other burrowing animals are a problem, hardware cloth or reinforcing wire mesh should be cut to size and placed on the soil surface under raised beds.

Where raised beds are built against the house or other structures, with the wall of the house serving as the back wall of the bed, care must be taken to waterproof the foundation wall as high as the level of the soil. There are several suitable waterproofing materials on the market and these can be found at larger building supply outlets.

The most expedient way to protect foundation walls from moisture damage is to add a back wall to the bed or planter to abut the structure. Even then, waterproofing the foundation wall is advisable to protect its integrity and French drains or other piping for carrying away drainage water should be installed under planters.

Raised beds with ample space between for wheelbarrow access. They run north and south so plants don't shade one another as they mature.

A difficult but successful reclamation of a steep hill. Interconnected terraced planters of redwood were built on flat planes cut out of the hillside. Access is by steps in the center.

RAISED BEDS FOR ORNAMENTALS

Unless raised beds will become part of the landscape design where they are intended to serve as bench seating, wall height is not a major consideration. Depending on the purpose they will serve, beds may be merely one brick or several feet high. Beds that flank garden walks are often only a few inches high and their main functions are to contain perimeter plants, to define the walkway, and to keep debris from the beds off the paving.

In areas where the native soil is excessively rocky or primarily clay, the two most commonly encountered problem soil conditions, beds are usually built higher—from

12″–18″. When filled with fertile loam, this depth provides enough growing room for roots to establish themselves before encountering the troublesome native soil underneath.

In areas where the soil is fertile and friable, there is no need to go to the expense of buying mixes or bulk topsoil simply to grow annuals, perennials, shrubs, and trees. If native soil is available on site for filling beds, it should be used. It can easily be amended to suit the tastes of particular species, such as acid-preference shrubs like rhododendrons (see Chapter 5).

A visually interesting planter design made with used brick on a concrete footing. An ample brick cap enables one to sit while tending plants.

INSTALLING IRRIGATION

Watering raised beds manually with a hose is a tedious chore that often must be done daily through the summer months, making one a slave to the garden. During vacations and other trips, arrangements must be made with friends or neighbors to fill in for you while you're away.

A far better solution is to install an automatic irrigation system that can be programmed to run for a specified period. This might be a system connected to lawn sprinkler lines or one utilizing a timer connected to an outdoor spigot that operates a drip irrigation system (see photo).

If you already have a sprinkler system, tee off the line and run PVC pipe to the raised bed(s). Install risers and full sprinkler heads or drip irrigation tubing to which you can

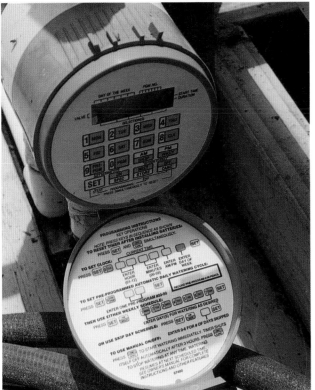

Upper left: Drip irrigation emitter delivers a steady, low volume of water directly to the root zones. Upper right: Raised bed gardens equipped with drip-irrigation tubing. Once plants mature, tubing will not be visible. Lower left: Automated timer for drip-irrigation system can be programmed as easily as controllers for automatic lawn sprinklers. Lower right: Several lines of "spaghetti" tubing can be connected to a drip-irrigation head to irrigate several plants at once.

Designing & Building Raised Beds

connect emitters on the surface of the finished beds.

Great strides have been made in drip irrigation technology in the last decade and the price of equipment has come down with the growing popularity of the system. Most garden centers and building supply outlets carry at least one brand. The concept is especially appealing to gardeners in areas where water shortages are frequent and rationing is a realistic possibility. Instead of wetting down several square feet of ground, including non-productive areas, and losing moisture to evaporation, drip emitters deliver water, drop by drop, precisely where it is needed— the root zone of plants. By inserting an emitter head (a dripper, mister, or sprayer) into the tubing at each plant location in the bed, that plant receives the lion's share of the irrigation water and there is very little waste.

Another benefit with drip irrigation is that it keeps moisture off foliage of plants that are subject to mildew, such as roses, cucumbers, squash, and tomatoes.

Construction Tips for Raised Beds

The same techniques used for building stationary planters apply in the construction of raised bed gardens. Footings for those made of mortared material must extend below the frost line in areas of seasonal hard freezes and those with walls that rise higher than three feet should be reinforced with rebars.

Like planters that become a major design element by their location, raised beds that dominate a front entry or other architectural focal point of the home should be constructed with the same material as the residence, finished the same color so that they blend with the house, or made with a complementary material, such as brick with white frame structures and native stone with Cape Cods.

Raised beds for crop plants are often made with decay-resistant lumber, rather than mortared materials. Like planters constructed of wood, these are easier and less expensive to erect and can be built so that they are simple to disassemble if this ever becomes desirable or necessary.

Once the irrigation system is in place, the quickest method of constructing wooden raised beds is to cut all the pieces to size and lay them out near the installation site. A typical raised planter will be built by attaching the sides and ends to corners 4×4's with rustproof screws. The sturdiest examples include 4×4's that extend a foot or so

Landscape timber sections, sunk on end to create a planter. Note rebar (reinforcing bar) stapled to timbers to provide stability against stress that soil weight exerts.

below the bottom of the bed. These extensions are then sunk into the ground at the four corners so the raised bed is anchored firmly in place. For raised beds longer than eight feet, install a 4×4' post in the middle on both sides to prevent the sides from bowing out.

One of the least expensive and easiest-to-build raised beds can be made using just two sheets of ¾" or 1" exterior plywood. These 4×8' panels may be cut down the center to yield side panels 2×8' and end boards can be cut across their width to provide boards 2×4'.

If a coping board for seating is desired, add a framework of 2×2" lumber below the rim to provide support and a surface for attaching fasteners.

These three photos show the various styles of raised bed planters that are commonly constructed. The style shown at the bottom is wheelchair-accessible.

Designing & Building Raised Beds

chapter 4

Plants, Shrubs & Trees for Above-Ground Gardens

Raised bed vegetable gardens can be quickly assembled with 2 × 6" or 2 × 8" dimension lumber and rust-proof fasteners.

Vegetables and other crop plants, as well as many ornamentals, are not limited to conventional garden plots; many can also be grown in containers and planters of appropriate size, as well as raised beds. The entire range of vegetables, including asparagus and corn, and all the bramble berries, prosper in large tubs and boxes, as do dwarf fruit trees which bear full-size fruit.

Planters, depending on their size and depth, are suitable for growing all the above, plus some of the deeper-rooted semi-dwarf and standard trees, as well as many specimen shrubs and trees.

(Page 56) *Charming patio garden created with hanging baskets, containers, and raised bed planters.*

(Previous page) *Camellias are excellent shrubs for containers and planters, although they need winter protection in the north.*

Raised beds that are open to the native soil can, of course, accommodate anything one wishes to grow, including standard size trees. The only caveat is that species which grow so tall they dwarf the raised bed and, consequently, appear out of scale to the bed should not be chosen. Instead, opt for those that don't grow taller than 30' at maturity.

Most fruit trees (and many ornamentals) are available as standards, semi-dwarfs, and dwarfs. The exception is *Pyrus*, for which no dwarf has as yet been developed.

Standards at maturity are about 20'–30' tall; semi-dwarfs are roughly half the size of standards, or 10'–15'; and dwarfs are approximately a third the size of standards, at 5'–8'.

Dwarf shrubs and trees prosper in large containers.

Instant color accents are easy with containers of blooming material. When the bloom cycle is over, pots can be moved to a less prominent spot.

Trees may be kept in containers for years if their roots are pruned every three to five years.

For containers and smaller planters, dwarf varieties adapt well, although growing standards and semi-dwarfs in confined quarters has a dwarfing effect on them. Standards normally do best in large planters and raised beds where their roots can roam freely.

When choosing varieties for containers and planters, select those that have the designation "nana" or "compacta" after their botanical name, if they are available. This indicates the specimen is a smaller cultivar and means the tree or shrub won't outgrow its container for many years to come, if at all.

Following are charts of plants, bulbs, shrubs and trees that may be grown in contained gardens, as well as lists of special-purpose shrubs and trees.

Like herbs, succulents generally have only a modest root structure and take readily to the confines of a container filled with a fast-draining mix.

VINING, CLIMBING, TRAILING PLANTS

Australian Bluebell Creeper (*Sollya heterophylla*)

Baltic Ivy (*Hedera helix 'Baltica'*)

Black-Eyed Susan (*Thunbergia alata*)

Burro Tail (*Sedum morganianum*)

Cape Plumbago (*Plumbago capensis*)

Chilean Bellflower (*Lapageria rosea*)

Christmas Cactus (*Schlumbergera bridgesii*)

Climbing Fern (*Lygodium palmatum*)

Climbing, Trailing Begonia (*Begonia scandens*)

Dwarf Bougainvillea (*Bougainvillea* hybrids)

Fern Asparagus (*Asparagus plumosus*)

Flowering Maple (*Abutilon megapotamicum*)

Glorybower (*Clerodendrum thomsoniae*)

Holly Fern (*Cyrtomium falcatum*)

Irish Ivy (*Hedera helix* 'Hibernica')

Ivy Geranium (*Pelargonium peltatum*)

Japanese Painted Fern (*Adiantum pedatum*)

Jasmine (*Jasminum* species)

Northern Maidenhair Fern (*Adiantum pedatum*)

Orange Clock Vine (*Thunbergia gregorii*)

Orchid Cactus (*Epiphyllum* hybrids)

Parrot's Beak (*Clianthus puniceus*)

Pittsburgh Ivy (*Hedera helix* 'Pittsburgh')

Southern Maidenhair Fern (*Adiantum capillus-veneris*)

Squirrel's Foot Fern (*Davallia trichomanoides*)

Trailing Fuchsia (*Fuchsia hybrida*)

Trailing Lantana (*Lantana montevidensis*)

Trailing Lobelia (*Lobelia erinus* 'Blue Cascade')

Trailing Nasturtium (*Tropaeolum* hybrids)

Trailing Phlox (*Phlox nivalis*)

Wax Plant (*Hoya carnosa*)

Wire Vine (*Muehlenbeckia complexa*)

FLOWERING AND FOLIAGE PLANTS FOR CONTAINERS

NAME	HEIGHT	BLOOMS	COLOR	DAYS TO GERMINATION	COMMENTS
ANNUALS					
Amethyst Flower *Browallia speciosa*	10″–24″	SU-FA	Blue, lavender-blue, white	14	Named varieties include 'Blue Bells', 'Silverbells', 'Sky Bells'.
Annual Phlox *Phlox drummondii*	6″–18″	SP	Yellow, blue, violet, red, pastels, white	14	Good named variety to try is 7″ 'Dwarf Beauty Mixed'.
Butterfly Flower *Schizanthus wisetonesis*	12″–18″	W-SP	Yellow, blue, pink, red, white, and multicolored	20–25	Set out after last frost. Prefers cool weather.
English Primrose* *Primula polyanthus*	5″–12″	SP	Almost all colors	21–40	Prefers cool weather with some shade. Named varieties include 'Clarke's', 'Santa Barbara' and 'Gold Laced'.
Garden Balsam *Impatiens balsamina*	24″–30″	SU	Yellow, salmon, purple, pink, rose, red, white	8–14	Named varieties include 'Double-Flowered Dwarf', 'Color Parade'.
Globe Candytuft *Iberis umbellata*	6″–15″	SP-SU	Salmon, lilac, pink, rose, red, white	10–15	Named dwarf varieties include 'Magic Carpet' and "Dwarf Jewel'.

Planters, Containers & Raised Beds

NAME	HEIGHT	BLOOMS	COLOR	DAYS TO GERMINATION	COMMENTS
Hyacinth-Flowered Candytuft *Iberis amara*	To 15"	SP-FA	White	16–20	Needs some shade in warm climates.
Johnny-Jump-Up* *Viola tricolor*	7"–10"	SP	Yellow, purple, white, and tricolored	10–20	Self sows.
Lobelia *Lobelia erinus*	4"–8"	SP-SU	Pale blue to deep purple and white	15–20	Good for edging a pot. Named varieties include 'Cambridge Blue', 'Crystal Palace', 'White Lady'.
Marigold *Tagetes* sp.	8"–36"	SU-FA	Yellow, gold, orange, red	5–8	Named varieties to try are dwarf 'Inca' and 'Guys and Dolls' or French marigold dwarf double 'Janie'.
Moss Rose *Portulaca grandiflora*	4"–8"	SU-FA	Yellow, orange, pink, rose, red, white, and pastels	14–28	Good for hanging baskets and window boxes. Named varieties include 'Afternoon Delight', 'Wax Pink', 'Sunglo' and 'Sunkiss'.
Nemesia *Nemesia strumosa*	8"–24"	SP-SU	All colors and bicolors except green	7–14	Named varieties include 'Carnival Blend' and 'Nana Compacta', a dwarf form.
Painted Nettle* *Coleus hybridus*	12"–24"	SU	Leaves are buff, brown, chartreuse, yellow, orange, salmon, green, purple, and red. Flowers are blue.	10–15	Does best in light shade. Named varieties include 'Carefree', 'Rainbow', 'Wizard'.
Pansy *Viola wittrockiana*	6"–8"	WI-SP	Yellow, apricot, blue, purple, rose, red, white, and bicolors	10–20	Two named varieties to try are 'Burgundy Lace' and 'Maxim Mixed'.
Petunia *Petunia hybrida*	10"–24"	SU	Yellow, blue, purple, pink, rose, red, white, and bicolors	8–10	Pinch back to keep compact. F1 hybrids are resistant to disease.
Pot Marigold *Calendula officinalis*	12"–24"	FA-SP or SP-SU***	Cream, yellow, apricot, orange, or red-orange	10–14	Dwarf strains include 'Bon Bon', 'Dwarf Gem' and 'Fiesta'.
Scarlet Sage* *Salvia splendens*	12"–30"	SU	Purple, pink, red, and white	12–15	Named varieties include 'Fiesta', 'Flare', 'Victoria', 'Oxford Blue'.
Snapdragon *Antirrhinum majus*	6"–36"	SP-SU	Bronze, orange, yellow, lavender, pink, rose, red, and white	10–14	Named varieties include 'Little Darling', 'Madame Butterfly', and a dwarf, 'Floral Carpet'.
Sweet Alyssum *Lobularia maritima*	6"–12"	SP-FA	Purple, lavender, pink, rose, white	18–15	

NAME	HEIGHT	BLOOMS	COLOR	DAYS TO GERMINATION	COMMENTS
Sweet Peas *Lathyrus odoratus*	36"–72"	SU	Blue, lavender, pink, red, white	10–14	Named varieties include 'Bijou', an easy heat-resistant bush type and 'Galaxy', a summer-blooming climber.
Sweet William** *Dianthus barbatus*	5"–12"	SU	Pink, rose, red and bicolors	5–10	
Verbena* *Verbena* sp.	8"–18"	SU	Blue, purple, pink, red, white	20–25	Named dwarf varieties include 'Amethyst', 'Blaze', 'Rainbow', 'Sparkle'.
Zinnia *Zinnia* sp.	4"–30"	SU-FA	Broad range of colors and bicolors	5–7	Named varieties include 'Buttons', 'Peter Pan', 'Ruffles', and 'Thumbelina', a dwarf variety.

PERENNIALS

NAME	HEIGHT	BLOOMS	COLOR	DAYS TO GERMINATION	COMMENTS
Basket of Gold *Aurinia saxatilis*	5"–15"	SP-SU	Yellow, gold	7–14	Excellent spreader.
Bedding Begonia *Begonia semperflorens*	6"–12"	SP-SU	Pink, red, white with bronze foliage	15–20	Long-lived blooms in shade.
Busy Lizzie *Impatiens wallerana* 'Blitz'	8"–30"	SP-SU	Orange, salmon, lavender, pink, red, white	15–20	Months of bloom in sheltered location. Pinch frequently to renew.
Common Aubrieta *Aubrieta deltoidea*	2"–6"	SP	Blue, lilac, rose, red	8–15	Good named variety is 'Novalis Blue'.
Cottage Pink *Dianthus plumarius*	10"–18"	SU-FA	Pink, rose, white, bicolor	5–10	A fragrant named variety is 'Spring Beauty'.
Creeping Jenny, Moneywort *Lysimachia nummularia*	24" (runners)	SU-FA	Yellow		Propagate by cuttings or division. Variety 'Aurea' has yellow leaves.
Dwarf Cup Flower *Nierembergia hippomanica violacea*	8"–12"	SU	Blue, purple, white	15–20	Two named varieties are 'Mont Blanc' and 'Purple Robe'.
Dwarf Periwinkle *Vinca minor*	To 24" (runners)	SP	Lavender-blue, white, and variegated foliage		Propagate by cuttings or division.
English Primrose *Primula polyanthus*	8"–12"	SP-SU	Yellow, apricot, orange, blue, pink, rose, red, white	15–25	Good choice for moist shade.
Evergreen Candytuft *Iberis sempervirens*	8"–18"	SP-SU	White	16–20	Compact named varieties include 'Little Gem', 'Purity', 'Snowflake'.
Flowering Tobacco *Nicotiana alata*	10"–30"	SU-FA	Lavender, pink, red, green, white	10–20	Named varieties include 'Metro Hybrid Series' and 'Sensation Mixed'.
Garden Zonal Geranium *Pelargonium hortorum*	18"–24"	SU-FA	Salmon, pink, rose, red	5–15	

NAME	HEIGHT	BLOOMS	COLOR	DAYS TO GERMINATION	COMMENTS
Italian Bellflower *Campanula isophylla*	12″–14″	SU-FA	Blue, white	14–20	Good for hanging basket. Protect in winter.
Ivy Geranium *Pelargonium peltatum*	Varies (trailer)	SU	Pastels and reds	5–15	Try named variety 'Summer Showers Hybrid Mixed'.
Madagascar Periwinkle* *Catharanthus roseus*	5″–15″	SP-FA	White with rose eye, blush, or rose pink	15–20	Excellent edging plant.
Nasturtium *Tropaeolum majus*	12″–96″ (trailer)	SU-FA	Yellow, orange, red, creamy white	7–12	Named varieties include 'Alaska' and 'Double Dwarf Jewel Mixed'.
Serbian Ballflower *Campanula porscharskyana*	12″–18″	SU	Blue, violet, white	14–21	Does well in part shade.
Trailing Campanula *Campanula fragilis*	8″–10″ (trailer)	SU	Blue, violet, white	14–21	Good for hanging baskets and window boxes.
Tuberous Begonia *Begonia × tuberhybrida*	24″–36″	SU	Apricot, yellow, coral	15–20	Lift in winter. Good hanger. Named varieties are 'Nonstop® Hybrid Mixed', 'Memory® Hybrid Mixed', 'Giant Cascade Double'.

*   = Annual or perennial, depending on region.   *** = Blooming time depends on region.
**   = Biennial or annual, depending on region.   1   = To 50 for scented varieties.

A wide array of bulbs, annuals, and perennials thrives in containers, as shown in these photos.

*Tuberous begonia (*Begonia tuberhybrida*)*

*Pansy (*Viola *sp.)*

Begonia 'Hawaiian Sunset'

ORNAMENTAL HERBS FOR CONTAINERS AND PLANTERS

NAME	TYPE	WHEN TO PLANT	HABIT, HEIGHT	PROPAGATION	COMMENTS
Angelica	Bi	Late summer	Upright, 5'–6'	Seeds	Give PM shade in hot summer climates.
Anise	A	Spring	Upright, 18"–24"	Seeds	Cut to ground when seeds change color.
Basil	A	Spring	Bushy, 7"–48"	Seeds	Dozens of new, colorful varieties.
Bay	Tree	Spring	Upright, to 30'	Rooted cuttings	Aromatic, decorative tree.
Bergamot	P	Spring	Upright, 24"–36"	Seeds	Give some shade in hot weather.
Bergamot, Wild	HP	Spring	Upright, 18"–36"	Seeds, transplants	Add lime to pot mix.
Borage	HHA	Spring or fall	Upright, 12"–24"	Seeds	Self-sows.
Caraway	Bi	Spring or late summer	Upright, 12"–24"	Seeds	Withhold water when flowers appear.
Catnip	HP	Spring	Bushy, 24"–36"	Seeds	Cut back plants to renew.
Chamomile, Roman	HHP	Spring	Bushy, 12"–18"	Seeds, cuttings	Prefers acid soil.
Chamomile, German	A	Spring or late fall	Upright, 18"–24"	Seeds	Add lime to soil mix.
Chervil	A	Spring	Cluster, 12"–24"	Seeds	For larger leaves, cut back flower heads before they set seed.
Chive	HP	Spring	Clumps, 8"–12"	Seeds, division	Fast spreader.
Cicely, Sweet	P	Spring or fall	Upright, 24"–36"	Seeds, division	Chill spring-planted seeds before sowing.
Coriander	HA	Spring	Upright, 24"–30"	Seeds	For seeds, wait until seed covering cracks.
Dill	A	Successive sowings all year	Upright, 24"–36"	Seeds	Self-sows.
Fennel, Sweet	HHP	Spring	Upright, 4'–6'	Seeds	Feed, prune regularly to enhance vigor.
Lavender	P	Spring	Bushy, 12"–30"	Seeds, cuttings	Very fragrant.
Lemon Balm	HHP	Spring	Clumps, 24"–30"	Seeds, divisions, cuttings	Cut back after bloom to prevent seed setting.
Lemongrass	P/A	Spring	Clumps, 4'–6'	Transplants	Move to shade if weather is 90°F+.
Lemon Verbena	ESH	Spring	Upright, 3'–4'	Transplants, softwood cuttings	Treat as annual or houseplant north of Zone 8.
Marjoram, Sweet	P	Spring	Clumps, 12"–24"	Transplants	Add lime to pot soil.
Mint, Apple	P/HP	Spring	Bushy, 24"–36"	Transplants, cuttings	Cut to ground at harvest.
Mint, Curly	HP	Spring	Bushy, 18"–24"	Transplants, cuttings	Cut to ground at harvest.
Mint, Pepper	HP	Spring or fall	Upright, 12"–24"	Transplants, cuttings	Invasive. Cut to ground twice during season.
Mint, Pineapple	HP	Spring or fall	Upright, 12"–24"	Transplants, cuttings	Head back severely at harvest.
Mint, Spear	HP	Spring	Upright, 24"–36"	Transplants, cuttings	Very invasive.
Oregano, Italian	TP	Spring	Upright, 12"–18"	Transplants, cuttings, division	Cut plants back when blooming begins.
Pennyroyal	HP	Spring	Upright, 12"–18"	Seeds, transplants, cuttings	Use sparingly in culinary dishes because of potential toxicity.
Rosemary	HHP	Spring	Bushy, 2'–5'	Seeds, tip cuttings	Use as a houseplant in cold-winter regions.
Sage	HP	Spring	Bushy, 12"–24"	Seeds	Grow in slightly acid soil.

Plants, Shrubs & Trees for Above-Ground Gardens

NAME	TYPE	WHEN TO PLANT	HABIT, HEIGHT	PROPAGATION	COMMENTS
Sage, Pineapple-scented	HHP/A	Spring	Upright, 3′–5′	Transplants, division	Use as houseplant in cold-winter areas.
Savory, Winter	HP	Spring	Upright, 8″–12″	Seeds	Grow in slightly acid soil.
Tarragon, French	HHP	Spring	Upright, 12″–24″	Transplants, division, tip cuttings	Needs winter dormancy. Cut to ground after frost.
Tarragon, Winter	HHP	Spring	Bushy, 12″–24″	Transplants, cuttings	Good indoor-outdoor plant.
Thyme	HP	Spring	Spreader, 2″–12″	Seeds, division, cuttings	Aromatic. Divide older plants to rejuvenate.
Woodruff, Sweet	HP	Spring	Spreader, 12″–18″	Transplants	Mix milled peat moss with potting soil. Keep mix moist.

A	= Annual	HHP/A	= Half hardy perennial grown as an annual
Bi	= Biennial	HP	= Hardy perennial
ESH	= Evergreen Shrub	P	= Perennial
HHA	= Half hardy annual	P/A	= Perennial grown as annual
HHP	= Half hardy perennial	TP	= Tender perennial

*Rosemary (*Rosmarinus officinalis*)*

BULBS, CORMS, RHIZOMES, AND TUBERS FOR CONTAINERS

NAME	PLANTING DEPTH	COLORS	HEIGHT	SEASON	WHEN TO PLANT
HARDY BULBS					
Allium *Allium* sp.	2"–6"	White, yellow, rose, lilac, blue, mixed	8"–5'*	Spring-Summer	Spring or fall*
Crocus *Crocus* sp.	2"–3"	White, yellow-orange, gold, lavender, violet, blue	2"–6"	Spring-Fall-Winter	Fall
Daffodil, Jonquil *Narcissus* sp.	6"–7"	White, yellow, and bicolors	12"–18"	Spring	Fall
Glory of the Snow *Chiondoxa* sp.	3"	Blue with white centers	6"–8"	Spring	Fall
Grape Hyacinth *Muscari* sp.	6"–7"	White, blue	4"–12"	Spring	Summer or fall
Hyacinth *Hyacinth* sp.	4"–6"	White, blue, and many pastel hues	8"–18"	Spring	Fall
Iris *Iris reticulata*	4"	White, yellow, violet, blue, purple	5"–6"	Winter-Spring	Fall
Lily *Lillium* sp.	6"	Many hues	12"–6'*	Spring-Summer	Fall or spring*
Snowdrop *Galanthus* sp.	4"	White with green accents	9"–12"	Winter-Spring	Fall
Squill *Scilla* sp.	2"–6"*	White, pink, blue, purple	3"–20"*	Spring-Summer	Summer or fall*
Tulip *Tulipa* sp.	4"–7"*	Many hues and color combinations	12"–26"*	Spring	Fall
Winter Daffodil *Sternbergia lutea*	4"–5"	Yellow	6"–9"	Fall	Summer
TENDER, HALF-HARDY BULBS					
Amaryllis *Hippeastrum* sp.	1"	White, pink, red, bicolors	12"–3'*	Spring-Summer	Spring
Begonia *Begonia tuberhybrida*	1"–2"	Many hues and pastels	8"–24"	Summer-Fall	Spring
Buttercup *Ranunculus asiaticus*	1"–2"	Many hues, including pastels	18"–24"	Summer	Spring
Caladium *Caladium* sp.	2"–3"	Leaves in many hues and combinations; flowers are pink	10"–12"	Spring-Summer	Spring
Calla *Zantedeschia* sp.	2"–6"[1]	White, yellow, pink	18"–4'*	Spring-Summer	Spring
Canna *Canna generalis*	2"–5"	Many hues, including bicolors	18"–6'*	Summer-Fall	Spring
Crinum *Crinum* sp.	Barely cover neck	White, pink, red	2'–3'	Summer-Fall	Spring

NAME	PLANTING DEPTH	COLORS	HEIGHT	SEASON	WHEN TO PLANT
Cyclamen *Cyclamen* sp.	1″	White, rose-pinks to salmon	4″–6″	Summer-Fall	Spring
Dahlia *Dahlia hybrida*	2″–3″	All except blue	1′–7′	Summer-Fall	Spring
Freesia *Freesia refracta*	2″	Yellow, orange, pink, purple	12″–18″	Summer	Spring
Gladiolus *Gladiolus* sp.	4″–6″	Many hues and color accents	24″–48″	Summer	Spring
Glory Lily *Gloriosa rothschildiana*	4″–5″	Yellow-and-scarlet	3′–5′	Summer	Spring
Harlequin Flower *Sparaxis tricolor*	3″–4″	White, yellow, red, and blues	12″–18″	Spring-Summer	Fall
Kaffir Lily *Clivia miniata*	Barely cover	White, yellow, orange, reds	12″–18″	Spring-Summer	Spring
Lily of the Nile *Agapanthus*	½″	White, blue, dark purple	1′–5′	Summer	Spring
Magic Flower *Achimenes*	½″–1″	Pink, lavender, blue, purple	18″–20″ (trailer)	Spring-Fall	Spring
Oxalis *Oxalis* sp.	2″–3″	Rose-pink to rose-purple	4″–6″	All seasons, depending on species	Spring
Pineapple Flower *Eucomis.*	6″	Multicolored	2′–3′	Summer	Spring
Tiger Flower *Tigrida pavonia*	1″–3″	White, yellow, orange, pink, red, lilac	16″–30″	Summer	Spring
Windflower *Anemone* sp.	1″–2″	White, red, violet, blue and mixed	7″–15″	Spring-Summer	Spring or fall*

* Depending on variety [1] Plant yellow and pink callas 2″ deep.

Fragrant hyacinths attractively grouped in half barrels.

VEGETABLES, BERRIES, AND FRUIT FOR CONTAINERS AND PLANTERS

VEGETABLE	SEASON	POT SIZE	PLANTS PER POT	SPACE BETWEEN PLANTS	EXPOSURE	MOISTURE	STAKE/ TRELLIS	DAYS TO HARVEST	COMMENTS
Artichoke	CS-WS	5 gal.	1	3'	S	EM		10–12 mos.	Protect in winter above Zone 8.
Asparagus	CS-WS	10 gal.	2	1'	S	SM		1–2 yrs.	Requires at least a year to produce edible spears. Start dormant root.
Beans									
Black-eyed Peas	WS	5 gal.	2	6"	S	EM		65–80	Side dress with 5-10-10 fertilizer.
Fava	CS	5 gal.	1	8"	S-PSH	EM	•	80–90	Suffers in hot weather.
Garbanzo	WS	5 gal.	1	8"	S	EM		90–105	Low yields per plant.
Lima (Bush)	WS	5–10 gal.	2–4	6"	S	EM		85–90	Direct sow in late spring.
Lima (Pole)	WS	5 gal.	2	6"	S	EM	•	85–90	'King of the Garden' is productive.
Snap (Bush)	CS	5–10 gal.	1–3	6"	S-PSH	EM		45–65	Harvest often.
Snap (Pole)	CS	5–10 gal.	2–4	6"	S-PSH	EM	•	65–70	Try 'Kentucky Wonder Resistant'.
Beets ('Detroit Dark Red', 'Early Wonder', 'Red Ace Hybrid')	CS	5 gal.	12	5"	S	SM		50–60	Thinning is important.
Broccoli ('DeRapa', 'Green Comet F1 Hybrid', 'Raab')	CS	5 gal.	2	14"	S-PSH	EM		60	Transplants hasten harvest time.
Brussels Sprouts ('Burpee Jade Cross E Hybrid', 'Dolmic F1 Hybrid', 'Long Island Improved')	CS	5 gal.	2	18"	S	EM		90+	Use transplants for earlier harvest. Take some small, tender sprouts.

Plant		Container		Spacing				Days	Notes
Cabbage ('Badger Market', 'Copenhagen Market', 'Golden Acre', 'Marion Market', 'Burpee's Surehead', 'Minicole F1 Hybrid')	CS	10 gal.	3	14"	S	EM		60–90	Feed a high nitrogen, high potash fertilizer three times during season.
Carrots ('Oxheart', 'Short 'n Sweet', 'Nantes', 'Orbit', 'Danvers Half Long', 'Autumn King Improved')	CS	5–10 gal.	10–20	2"	S	EM		60–75	Thinning seedlings is crucial.
Cauliflower ('Early Snowball', 'Snow Crown', 'Super Snowball')	CS	5 gal.	3	14"	S	EM		55–70	Protect from heat stress and keep well watered.
Celery ('Giant Pascal', 'Tall Utah 52–70R Improved', 'Ventura')	CS	10 gal.	5	10"	S-PSH	EM		90–120	Mound soil around base of plants.
Corn, Sweet ('Extra Early Sweet', 'F-M Cross', 'Precocious')	WS	10–15 gal.	4–8	12"	S	EM		65–80	Ask your nurseryman about local varieties.
Cucumber ('Burpee Hybrid II', 'Bush Champion', 'Salad Bush Hybrid', 'Victory')	WS	5–10 gal.	1–2	10"	S	EM	•	50–65	Take cukes when young and tender.
Eggplant ('Asian Bride', 'Bambino', 'Black Magic', 'Dusky Hybrid', 'Jersey King')	WS	10 gal.	3–4	18"	S	EM	•	70–90	Start with transplants for earlier harvest.
Leeks ('Broad London', 'Cortina', 'Titan')	CS	5–10 gal.	18–24	3"	S-PSH	EM		75–90	Use 1 lb. of bone meal in container mix.
Lettuce ('Baby Bibb', 'Fordhook', 'Paris White Cos', 'Red Sails')	CS	5–10 gal.	4–8	8"	S-PSH	EM		30–65	Protect in hot weather with shade cloth.

Plants, Shrubs & Trees for Above-Ground Gardens

VEGETABLE	SEASON	POT SIZE	PLANTS PER POT	SPACE BETWEEN PLANTS	EXPOSURE	MOISTURE	STAKE/TRELLIS	DAYS TO HARVEST	COMMENTS
Melons (CANTALOUPE: 'Ambrosia Hybrid', 'Burpee Hybrid', 'Bush Star Hybrid', 'Sweetheart F1 Hybrid'; HONEYDEW: 'Amber Green', 'A-One Hybrid'; WATERMELON: 'Bush Baby', 'Bush Sugar Baby', 'Fordhook Hybrid', 'Yellow Baby Hybrid')	WS	5–15 gal.	1-2	12"	S	EM		75–100	Mini-melons mature earlier than standards.
Okra ('Blondy', 'Burgundy', 'Clemson Spineless')	WS	5 gal.	1	18"	S	EM	•	45–60	Mulch topsoil with black plastic for soil warmth.
Onion/Garlic (ONION: 'Evergreen Bunching', 'Italian Red Bottle', 'Sweet Sandwich F1 Hybrid'; GARLIC: Use market bulbs.)	CS	5 gal.	8–10	3"	S	EM		90–120	Feed bi-monthly.
Peas (BUSH: 'Burpee's Blue Bantam', 'Dwarf Gray Sugar', 'Morse's Progress No. 9'; TALL: 'Alderman', 'Melting Sugar', 'Wando')	CS	10 gal.	10–14	3"	S	SM	•	60–85	Use low-nitrogen fertilizer.
Peppers, Bell ('Bell Boy', 'Purple Beauty', 'Select California Wonder', 'Sweet Chocolate'; DWARF: 'Jingle Bells', 'Little Dipper Hybrid')	WS	3–5 gal.	1	18"	S	EM	•	60–85	Harvest often to keep peppers coming.
Potatoes ('Charlotte', 'Irish Cobbler', 'Kennebec'; NOVELTY: 'All Blue', 'Bintje', 'Blossom')	WS	15–20 gal.	8–10	7"	S	EM		85–95	Cover stems with peat moss as they grow.

Plant	Season	Container	No.	Spacing	Light			Days	Notes
Radish ('Cherry Belle', 'China Rose', 'Crunchy Red F1 Hybrid', 'White Chinese')	CS	2–10 gal.	16–36	1½"	S	EM		15–45	Thin seedlings and make successive plantings.
Spinach ('America', 'Bloomsdale Long-Standing', 'Hybrid No. 7', 'Vienna Hybrid')	CS	10 gal.	6–8	6"	S-PSH	EM		35–60	Take tender young leaves periodically.
Squash (SUMMER: Burpee's Fordhook Zucchini', 'Clairimore Lebanese', 'Pasta Hybrid', 'Pic-N-Pic Hybrid', 'Sunburst Hybrid'; WINTER: 'Burpee's Butterbush', 'Bush Acorn Table King', 'Cream of the Crop', 'Orangetti F1 Hybrid')	WS	10 gal.	2	12"	S	EM	•	50–120	Use black plastic mulch to keep soil warm.
Swiss Chard ('Fordhook Giant', 'Rhubarb', 'Ruby')	CS	5–10 gal.	2–4	6"	S-PSH	EM		50–65	Feed bimonthly until harvest.
Tomato (FOR CONTAINERS: 'Basket King Hybrid', 'Golden Pigmy', 'Patio Prize' VFN, 'Red Cherry', 'Tiny Tim', 'Tom Thumb'); FOR PLANTERS: (All the above plus 'Beefsteak', 'Early Girl', 'Super Marmande', 'Tigerella')	WS	5–20 gal.	1	24"	S	EM	•	50–100	Mix two tablespoons pelletized limestone per gallon of soil.
Turnip/Rutabaga TURNIP: ('Just Right F1 Hybrid', 'Purple-Top', 'White Globe', 'Tokyo Cross'); RUTABAGA: ('American Purple Top', 'Burpee's Purple-Top Yellow')	CS	15–20 gal.	12–16	6"	S	EM		40–60	Feed only once, a week after thinning.

BERRIES

VEGETABLE	SEASON	POT SIZE	PLANTS PER POT	SPACE BETWEEN PLANTS	EXPOSURE	MOISTURE	STAKE/ TRELLIS	DAYS TO HARVEST	COMMENTS
Blueberries HIGHBUSH: ('Bluecrop', 'Blueray', 'Jersey'); RABBITEYE: ('Centurion', 'Delight', 'O'Neal', 'Tifblue')	CS-WS	10–15 gal.	1	36"	S-PSH	EM		60–120	Use an acid soil mix rich in peat moss.
Currants/Gooseberries CURRANTS (Reds: 'Fay's Prolific', 'Improved Perfection', 'Red Lake'; Whites: 'White Grape', 'White Imperial'); GOOSEBERRIES: ('Careless', 'Pixwell', 'Downing')	CS-WS	10–15 gal.	1	36"	S-PSH	EM	*	60–120	Don't feed plants the first year.
Blackberries ('Brazor', 'Ebony King', 'Lawton', 'Raven')	CS	15–20 gal.	1–2	36"	S	EM	•	60–90	Erect types are best for containers.
Raspberries (Reds: 'Canby' (thornless), 'Heritage', 'Killarney'; Yellows: 'Fallgold'; 'Golden Queen'; Purples: 'Purple Autumn', 'Royalty'; Black: 'New Improved Cumberland', 'New Logan')	CS	15–20 gal.	1	36"	S	EM	•	60–90	Everbearers bear second crop in fall.
Strawberries ('Shortcake', 'Earliglow', 'Lateglow', 'Royalty', 'Ruegen Improved' (Alpine), 'Yellow Wonder' (Alpine, sweet yellow); Zones 9–10 varieties: 'Aptos', 'Douglas', 'Hecker', 'Sequoia', 'Tioga')	CS	3–5 gal.	2–8	8"	S-PSH	EM		30–65	True everbearers produce three seasonal crops.

Planters, Containers & Raised Beds

FRUIT

Plant	Season	Container		Light	Moisture	Days	Comments
Apples (Dwarf Trees) ('Empire', 'Garden Delicious', 'Gibson Yellow Delicious', 'Red Delicious'; LOW CHILL VARIETIES: 'Anna', 'Beverly Hills', 'Dorsett Golden', 'Winter Banana')	CS-WS	15–25 gal.	1	S	EM	Varies	Most apples thrive in Zones 5–8 and need a pollinator.
Apricots (Dwarf Trees) ('Flora Gold', 'Garden Annie', 'Moorpark')	W/S	15–20 gal.	1	S	EM	90–120	Apricots are adapted to conditions in Zones 6–9.
Figs ('Brown Turkey', 'Mission', 'Peter's Honey', 'Texas Ever-bearing')	W/S	15–20 gal.	1	S	EM	90–120	Cultivars listed are self-fruitfuls. Need winter protection above Zone 8.
Peaches (Dwarf Trees) (EARLY: 'Red Haven'; MIDSEASON: 'Bonanza II', 'Honey Babe'; LATE: 'Belle of Georgia', 'Compact Red Haven')	W/S	15–20 gal.	1	S	EM	Varies	Peaches may be grown in Zones 5–9. Most are self fruitful.
Pears ('Bartlett', 'Bosc', 'Clapp's Favorite', 'Kieffer', 'Seckel')	W/S	15–20 gal.	1	S	EM	90–120	Most pears prosper in Zones 5–8 and need a pollinator.
Plums (JAPANESE: 'Abundance', 'Methley', 'Bruce', 'Burbank', 'Santa Rosa'; EUROPEAN: 'Stanely')	W/S	15–20 gal.	1	S	EM	90–120	Most plums prosper in Zones 5–9. Nearly all Japanese varieties need a pollinator.

CS = Cool Season
W/S = Warm Season
CS-WS = Cool Season to Warm Season
S = Sun

PSH = Part Shade
EM = Evenly Moist
SM = Slightly Moist

The handsome examples of contained crop gardens. Upper left shows a thriving raised bed garden where sweet corn is the primary crop. Upper right is a grouping of half whiskey barrels filled with salad crops and some corn, grown mostly for its decorative appeal. Lower left is a boxed small-scale greens garden.

Apple 'Beverly Hills', left, and peach (Prunus persica) *are both dwarf fruit trees that thrive in large (5+ gallon) containers. They need full sun through the season to set buds and fruit.*

SHRUBS FOR CONTAINERS AND PLANTERS

NAME	EVERGREEN/ DECIDUOUS	FLOWERS	COLORS	SHADE/SUN	HEIGHT	ZONES
Azalea *Rhododendron* sp.	Both*	•	White, pink, red, lilac, purple	Both	Varies*	4–10
Boxwood *Buxus* sp.	Both*			S/PSH	10′–20′	6–10
Camellia *Camellia* hybrids	E	•	White, pink, red, and combinations	Both	7′–45′*	7–10
Cornelian Cherry *Cornus mas*	D	•	Yellow	S	15′–20′	5–9
Crape Myrtle *Lagerstroemia indica*	D	•	White, pink, rose, red, purple, lavender	S	To 30′	7–9
English Lavender *Lavandula angustifolia*	E	•	Lavender, purple	S	1′–4′	6–10
Flowering Quince *Chaenomeles speciosa;* *C. × superba*	D	•	White, pink, orange	S	5′–10′	5–10
Forsythia *Forsythia* sp.	D	•	Yellow	S/PSH	12″–10′*	5–9
Fuchsia *Fuchsia* sp.	E	•	Many colors and combinations	S/PSH	Trailer	9–10
Glossy Abelia *Abelia grandiflora*	Both*	•	White, pinkish-white	S	3′–6′	6–8
Heavenly Bamboo *Nandina domestica*	E			S/PSH	3′–8′	6–8
Hinoki False Cypress *Chamaecyparis obtusa*	E			S/PSH	7′–10′	8–10**
Hydrangea *Hydrangea* sp.	Both*	•	White, pink, lavender, blue	S/PSH	3′–20′*	5–10*
Juniper *Juniper* sp.	E			S	Dwarfs to tree forms	4–10*
Lilac, Persian *Syringa × persica*	D	•	Pale lilac	S	5′–6′	4–8
Mugo Pine *Pinus mugo mugo*	E			S/PSH	2′–10′	3–9**
Oleander *Nerium oleander*	E	•	White, yellow, salmon, pink, red	S	10′–30′	8–10
Oregon Grape Holly *Mahonia aquifolium*	E	•	Lavender, purple	S/PSH	3′–6′	5–10**
Paper Flower *Bougainvillea*	E	•	Many hues	S	Varies	9–10
Photinia *Photinia* sp.	E	•	White	S/PSH	5′–12′	7–10
Podocarpus *Podocarpus* sp.	E			S/PSH	To 50′	9–10

NAME	EVERGREEN/ DECIDUOUS	FLOWERS	COLORS	SHADE/SUN	HEIGHT	ZONES
Purpleleaf Barberry *Berberis thunbergii* 'Atropurpurea'	D			S	4'–6'	4–8
Rhododendron *Rhododendron* sp.	Both*	•	Many hues, including orange	S/PSH	To 25'*	4–10*
Rose *Rosa* sp.	Both*	•	Many hues, bicolors	S	Varies greatly	5–10
Silverberry *Eleaegnus pungens*	E	•	Silver-white	S	To 15'	7–9
Spindle Tree *Euonymus europaea*	D		Colorful foliage, fruit	S/PSH	8'–20'*	3–9
Spiraea *Spiraea* sp.	D	•	White, pink, red	S	2'–9'*	3–9*
Sweet Olive *Osmanthus fragrans*	E	•	Greenish-white	S/PSH	To 10'	9–10
Viburnum *Virburnum* sp.	Both*	•	White, pink	S/PSH	3'–20'*	3–10*
Wintercreeper *Euonymus fortunei radicans*	E			S/PSH	Trailer	6–10
Weigela *Weigela* sp.	D	•	White, red	S	3'–8'	4–9

*	= Depending on variety	D	= Deciduous
**	= Except desert regions of west	S	= Sun
E	= Evergreen	PSH	= Part Shade

Big-leaf hydrangea (Hydrangea macrophylla*)*

Azalea (Rhododendron *sp.*)

Plants, Shrubs & Trees for Above-Ground Gardens

Planters, Containers & Raised Beds

*Opposite page: weigela (*Weigela florida*). Above left: mahonia (*Mahonia aquifolium *'Compacta'*). Above right: Japanese spiraea (*Spiraea japonica*).*

TREES FOR CONTAINERS AND PLANTERS

NAME	EVERGREEN DECIDUOUS	FLOWERS	COLORS	SHADE/SUN	HEIGHT	ZONES
Amur Maple *Acer ginnala*	D	•	Yellow	S	To 20'	2
Dogwood *Cornus florida*	D	•	White, yellow, pink, red	S/PSH	20'–40'	5–9
Dwarf Alberta Spruce *Picea glauca* 'Conica'	E			S	6'–10'	3–6
Eastern Redbud *Cercis canadensis*	D	•	White, pink, or purple	S	To 35'	5–8
Evergreen Pear *Pyrus kawakami*	E/D**	•	White	S/PSH	To 30'	9–10
Flowering Plum *Prunus cerasifera* 'Thundercloud'	D	•	White, pink	S	To 25'	5–9
Ginkgo *Ginkgo biloba*	D			S	30'–45'	4–10
Japanese Flowering Crab Apple *Malus floribunda*	D	•	Pale pink	S	To 25'	4–8
Japanese Maple *Acer palmatum*	D			S/PSH	15'–20'	5–8 (east) 6–9 (west)**
Loquat *Eribotrya japonica*	E	•	White	S	To 30'	8–10
Meyer Lemon *Citrus* sp.	E	•	White	S	7'–9'	9–10
Sargent Crab Apple *Malus sargentii*	D	•	White (pink buds)	S	12'–14'	5–8
Saucer Magnolia *Magnolia soulangiana*	D	•	White, pinkish-white, purple	S/PSH	18'–25'	5–10
Star Magnolia *Magnolia stellata*	D	•	White	S/PSH	8'–10'	5–10
Sweet Bay *Laurus nobilis*	E			S/PSH	12'–20'	9–10
Trident Maple *Acer buergeranum*	D			S	15'–20'	5–8 (east) 6–9 (west)

NAME	EVERGREEN DECIDUOUS	FLOWERS	COLORS	SHADE/SUN	HEIGHT	ZONES
Washington Thorn *Crataegus phaenopyrum*	D	•	White	S	To 30'	5–9
Weeping Fig *Ficus benjamina*	E			S/PSH	To 50'	9–10
Yew Pine *Podocarpus macrophyllus*	E			S/PSH	To 50'	7–10

*	= Depending on variety	D	= Decidious
**	= Depending on region grown	S	= Sun
E	= Evergreen	PSH	= Part Shade

Japanese maple (Acer palmatum*)*

Eley crab apple (Malus purpurea *'Eleyi'*)

*Silk oak (*Grevillea robusta*)*

PLANTS FOR PORTABLE PRIVACY AND SHADE

NAME	EVERGREEN/ DECIDUOUS	SPECIAL FEATURE	AVERAGE HEIGHT/WIDTH	ZONES**
SHRUBS				
Alpine Currant *Ribes alpinum*	D	Scarlet fruit	8'/6'	3–7
Bamboo *Bambusa* and other species	E		Varies	8–10
Big Leaf Hydrangea *Hydrangea macrophylla*	D	Pink, blue flowers in summer	6'/6'	6–10
Bougainvillea, Paper Flower *Bougainvillea* hybrids	E	Colorful bracts in vibrant colors	Varies	9–10
Camellia *Camellia* hybrids	E	White, pink, red, bicolor flowers, spring to summer	25'/8'	7–9
Chinese Hibiscus *Hibiscus rosa-sinensis*	E	Pink to red, yellow to orange flowers in summer	15'/10'	9–10
Chinese Holly *Ilex cornuta*	E	Red berries	15'/12'	7–10
Cleyera *Cleyera japonica*	E	Small white flowers, red berries, spring	15'/15'	7–9
Drooping Leucothoe *Leucothoe fontanesiana* and *L. f.* 'Scarletta'	E	White flowers in clusters in spring	6'/6'	5–9
Father Hugo's Rose *Rosa hugonis*	D	Yellow flowers in spring	8'/6'	5–9
Flowering Currant *Ribes sanguineum*	D	Red flowers, bluish-black fruit, spring-summer	10'/7'	6–8
Glossy Abelia *Abelia grandiflora*	E/D	White flowers June to October	8'/5'	6–8
Holly Osmanthus, Sweet Olive *Osmanthus fragrans*	E	White fragrant flowers in fall	15'/12'	7–9
Japanese Holly *Ilex crenata*	E		10'/8'	6–10
Japanese Spirea *Spiraea japonica*	D	White, pink blooms in spring	9'/9'	4–10
Oregon Grape Holly *Mahonia aquifolium*	E	Yellow fragrant blooms, bluish fruit in spring	6'/4'	5–10
Ornamental Grasses (Various species)	E/D		Varies	5–10
Pomegranate *Punica granatum*	D	Orange-red flowers, edible fruit in spring	15'/10'	8–10
Rhododendron *Rhododendron* sp.	E/D	Blooms in many hues in spring	25'/20'	4–10
Rosemary *Rosmarinus officinalis*	E	Pale blue flowers fall to winter	6'/6'	7–10

NAME	EVERGREEN/ DECIDUOUS	SPECIAL FEATURE	AVERAGE HEIGHT/WIDTH	ZONES**
Rugosa Rose *Rosa rugosa*	D	White, red blooms in summer	6'/4'	3–8
Silverberry *Elaeagnus pungens*	E	Silver-white flowers, oval red fruit spring-summer	15'/8'	8–9
Snowmound Spirea *Spiraea nipponica* 'Snowmound'	D	White flowers in clusters in spring	6'/6'	4–9
Weigela *Weigela florida*	D	White, pink, red flowers in spring	8'/6'	4–8
TREES				
Amur Maple *Acer ginnata*	D	Red fall color	20'/12'	2–8
Apple Serviceberry *Amelanchier grandiflora*	D	Pink flowers in spring	20'/15'	4–8
Flowering Crab Apple *Malus* 'Coralburst', 'Donald Wyman'	D	White, rose-pink flowers in spring	20'/15'	4–9
Pineapple Guava *Feijoa sellowiana*	E	Unusual flowers in spring, edible fruit in summer. Prune to tree form.	20'/10'	8–10
Red Flowering Dogwood *Cornus florida rubra*	D	Red blooms in spring	25'/10'	5–9
Sargent Crab Apple *Malus sargentii*	D	White flowers in spring	15'/8'	5–8
Silk Oak *Grevillea robusta*	E	Orange flowers in spring	10'/5'	9–10
Star Magnolia *Magnolia stellata*	D	White blooms in spring	10'/4'	5–10
Sweet Bay *Laurus nobilis*	E	Aromatic foliage	25'/10'	8–10
Weeping Fig *Ficus benjamina*	E		25'/20'	10
Yew Pine *Podocarpus macrophyllus*	E		15'/8'	8–10

*	= Height and width given for container-grown shrubs, trees	E	= Evergreen
**	= Scrubs, trees wintered indoors can be grown in colder zones	D	= Deciduous
		E/D	= Evergreen or deciduous, depending on region grown

*Chinese hibiscus (*Hibiscus rosa-sinensis)*, above;
sweet bay (*Laurus nobilis)*, below.*

Planters, Containers & Raised Beds

*Dwarf pomegranate (*Punica granatum *'Nana'),
above left; bamboo (*Bambusa *sp.), upper right;
Pineapple guava (*Feijoa sellowiana*), lower right.*

Soil Mixes & Fertilizers for Contained Gardens

Clay sewer pipes filled with improved soil make excellent planters.

By choosing various lengths of pipe, you can create a staggered height effect as shown here.

ell-balanced soil mixes for containers, planters and raised beds hold the key to the success or failure of these gardens. Just as people of different cultures have developed an ethnic or regional diet, many plant species have adapted to their own specific preferences. For example, Rhododendrons, gardenias, and blueberries thrive in acid soil, which is one that is rich in organic matters such as peat moss and oak

---

(Page 90) A well-designed raised bed garden filled with bountiful crops, flowers.

(Previous page) Herb planters are filled with a specially formulated mix ideal for herb culture.

leaf mold. If these species are grown in a high pH alkaline medium, they will demonstrate their displeasure by producing chlorotic foliage, sparse and stunted flowers that drop at a touch and, in the case of blueberries, modest (if any) fruit set.

First of all, you should understand what pH is and why it is important in the culture of plants. It really isn't all that technical. The relative acid content of soil can be measured on what is called a pH scale. This scale spans 1 to 14, with 7.0 being neutral, or evenly balanced between acidity and alkalinity. A reading below 7.0 indicates the soil sample is acidic; anything above 7.0 means it is alkaline.

You can test your own mixes with pH test kits sold at many garden centers. By adding peat moss, leaf mold, and homemade or commercial compost, you can acidify alkaline soil. Conversely, by mixing in agricultural lime, you can change acid media into alkaline. By repeating the test after each blending, you can keep track of how alkaline or how acid the mix is.

Most vegetables produce best in a soil that is slightly alkaline to neutral. Among these are beans, beets, cabbage, cantaloupe, cauliflower, celery, cucumbers, lettuce, onions, peas, rhubarb, and squash. Knowing this, you can blend a mix that is ideally suited to growing prize-winning vegetables.

"SOILLESS," SYNTHETIC MIXES

Based on research at two prestigious universities, soilless plant mix formulas were developed that provide the container gardener with superior planting media. Popularly referred to as synthetic mixes, they are composed of a number of organic ingredients including ground peat moss, vermiculite, perlite, ground limestone, sand, fertilizer, and wood products.

Good garden loam—friable and nutrient-rich.

Soilless mixes are easy to make and are also available premixed and packaged at many garden centers. Some of these may be lacking ingredients that should be added. Check labels for contents.

Their primary benefits over conventional garden soil are that they are lightweight and easy for plant roots to colonize and that they are free of the common problems garden loam is heir to: weed seeds, soil-borne disease pathogens and destructive insects.

Another advantage is that it is easier to custom-blend mixes to suit the tastes of specific species. If, for example, acid-preference plants will be grown in it, the pH level can be lowered by adding additional peat or leaf mold. In vegetable gardens, if root crops like peanuts, potatoes, radishes, and sweet potatoes are the primary crop plants, more peat can be mixed in to provide the extra acidity these plants prefer (4.0–5.5 pH). This acidity level is also tailor-made for most berries—blackberry, blueberry, cranberry, and huckleberry.

Soilless mixes may include chicken manure, steer manure, vermiculite, sand, peat, compost, loam, and gypsum.

Soil test kits are fairly reliable guides to determining nutrient deficiencies in soil. Shown is a basic home gardener's kit.

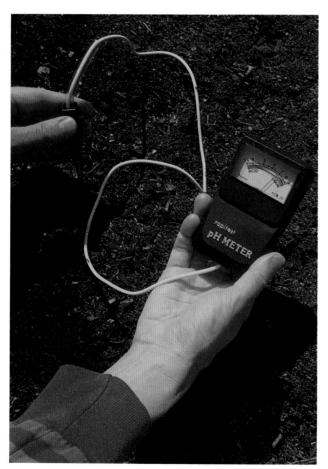

Meters measuring the pH value of soil are useful in creating custom mixes.

Soilless mixes are sold as "potting soil" under a variety of trade names in bags from two-quarts size to four-cubic-feet capacity. If you have only a few containers or small planters to fill, this is the most economical way to go. But, if there are large planters and raised beds to fill, the most cost effective method would be to have a load of topsoil delivered. In most cities, firms that offer this service are listed in the yellow pages of the telephone directory under "Soil" or "Topsoil." The typical cost for a cubic yard of soil is $16 delivered and there is usually a minimum volume requirement to avoid a delivery surcharge. If you pick up the topsoil at the outlet, the cost is about half the delivered rate. The average pickup truck bed holds from 2 to 2½ cubic yards.

What do you get when you buy soil from a bulk dealer? This depends on the source. Some who are offering topsoil are actually selling compost. This may be mushroom-based, which is the waste from a mushroom farming operation, or manure-based. Both are rich in nutrients and may contain some organic additives such as straw, sawdust, or wood shavings. Others may sell actual soil from construction excavations and other sources that has been enriched with organic matter and composted for months to produce a fertile mix that approximates naturally formed topsoil.

If the only bulk mix available is compost, this is fine for planters and beds, provided it has been aged, it is free of weed seeds and disease pathogens and you know what it contains so you can add amendments to blend special mixes.

Most packaged mixes are steam sterilized to kill harmful organisms and weed seeds. Soil bought in bulk probably won't be since it is often composted in open fields. If the bulk soil you buy contains barnyard manures, it should be composted for a few weeks to dilute the potency and bouquet of the manures. Ask your source what ingredients are in their soil or compost and how long it has been composted. Proper composting usually kills most or all of the noxious weed seeds.

For rooftop and balcony gardens, where weight is sometimes a concern, soilless mixes are the ideal media. On average, building codes require a residential balcony to sustain 60 lbs. per square foot and a rooftop to support even greater loads. An 8 × 12′ balcony, for example, must

Composting garden and kitchen waste is growing in popularity. A good medium-sized type for small gardens is this tumbler model.

One of the oldest known organic amendments and fertilizers is steer manure. It is available deodorized (buy only naturally, not chemically, deodorized types) and composted.

handle 5,760 lbs., or approximately 41 people with an average weight of 140 lbs. Even a dozen large lightweight containers and planters filled with plants in soilless mixes would not begin to approach this load limit.

Blending Your Own Planting Mixes

When a special soil mix formula is needed, or if you buy topsoil in bulk, you will need to add the amendments that create mixes suitable for what you want to grow. Many amendments are also used singly or in combination as mulches, which will be explored a bit later.

Specific mix recipes are included later in this chapter. First, if you aren't sure what the various amendments are and what they contribute to a fertile, productive planting mix, study the following:

COMPOST is decomposed vegetable matter that is filled with beneficial microorganisms and is very nutrient-rich.

FIR BARK When ground to a fine consistency, fir bark adds humus to the soil. Look for bark that has been nitrogen-stabilized so it does not draw nitrogen from the soil to aid in the decomposition process.

LEAF MOLD that is ground so it blends well with other ingredients is an excellent substitute for the costlier peat

Mini kitchen gardens of salad greens and herbs fit on any sunny terrace or patio.

moss and performs a similar function—adding acidity and bulk.

MANURE, STEER In addition to adding bulk to the soil, manure contributes some nitrogen nutrition to plants. Avoid, if you can, manures that have been deodorized chemically since these chemicals can damage plant tissue. With packaged commercial manures, deodorizing methods may not be recorded.

PEAT MOSS comes from ancient bogs and is primarily decomposed vegetable matter that is high in acid content. It must be soaked thoroughly before it is mixed for it to become water-absorbent.

PERLITE is volcanic rock that is ground, then heated, which causes it to expand to almost 20 times its original volume. It doesn't absorb moisture, but moisture clings to its surface.

SAND is composed of either quartz or mineral fragments and is excellent as an ingredient in mixes to help keep the soil open for root penetration and for efficient drainage.

SAWDUST, REDWOOD adds to the structure and openness of a mix. It should be naturally fortified with nitrogen, not enriched with chemical-sourced nitrogen.

VERMICULITE is a mineral which, like perlite, expands several times its original volume when subjected to extreme heat. It absorbs water and helps mixes retain their moisture content for longer periods.

Following are several general and crop-specific soilless mixes that are popular with gardeners:

Lightweight Mix
(For rooftop, balcony gardens)
   2 gallons vermiculite
   2 gallons perlite
   1 gallon coarsely ground peat moss (damp)
   2 gallons packaged soil or compost

Standard Mix/Vegetables
Where combined weight is no problem, a standard mix containing some horticultural grade or sharp builder's

Where soil is rocky or infertile, a "boxed" garden such as this filled with a custom soilless mix will produce bountiful crops or flowers.

sand is recommended. Compost is cheaper by volume than peat moss, so you can save substantially on planter media by buying compost or topsoil in bulk and blending your own mixes.

If you are preparing only a few containers, the easiest method is to buy commercially packaged mixes that contain the appropriate amendments. These are usually listed on the bag. The desirable amendments, as described above, are perlite, vermiculite and sphagnum or peat moss.

If you are mixing bulk materials for growing vegetables, use this recipe:

5 gallons compost

1 gallon horticultural grade or sharp builder's sand

1 gallon vermiculite or perlite

1 gallon coarsely ground peat moss

Add 2 cups of a complete organic fertilizer to the bottom third layer of mix in the container or planter and blend well.

Standard Mix/Annuals, Perennials

2 gallons finely ground peat moss

1 gallon compost

1 gallon sharp builder's sand

1 cup dolomite limestone

½ cup organic fertilizer

Standard Mix/Shrubs, Trees

2 gallons ground fir bark or nitrogen-stabilized redwood

sawdust

1 gallon sharp builder's sand

1 gallon coarsely ground peat moss

1 cup ground limestone

Standard Mix/Herbs

Many herbs do surprisingly well in lean, unimproved soil, but like most other plants, flourish in a medium containing fertile humus. In the main, herbs prefer a neutral or

Porch accents such as this antique horse-drawn basket filled with hydrangeas add a cheerful touch to an entry.

Purple-leaf plum (Prunus cerasifera 'Atropurpurea')

As mentioned earlier, herbs thrive in containers of all sizes. This planting, when mature, will fill this large-capacity pot.

slightly alkaline medium that drains well. A mix that has proven successful for many herb-growers is:

1 gallon compost

1 gallon ground peat moss

2 gallons sharp builder's sand

(For growing angelica, lovage, and mint, add 2 cups of vermiculite to the recipe)

Planting Mixes for Fruits, Berries

Dwarf stone fruit trees need a mix that is lightweight, retains some moisture, yet drains well. This means the soilless mixes. There are dozens of special fruit/berry mixes on the market and these are often available at large garden shops.

To mix your own blend, combine the following ingredients:

9 cubic feet (72 gallons) sharp builder's sand

9 cubic feet ground fir or pine bark (nitrogen-stabilized)

5 lbs organic fertilizer containing chelated trace elements

9 cubic feet compost

5 lbs dolomite limestone

CITRUS roots decline when there is too much free water around them, so a mix that drains efficiently is essential:

2 gallons ground fir bark

1 gallon nitrogen-stabilized redwood sawdust

1 gallon compost

1 gallon sharp builder's sand

BERRIES thrive in a humus-rich mix. Blackberries, blueberries, currants, gooseberries, huckleberries and raspberries do well in a medium that is somewhat acidic (4.0–5.5 pH):

2 gallons coarsely ground peat moss

1 gallon ground fir bark

1 gallon well-rotted (composted) manure

1 gallon sharp builder's sand

(For blueberries, increase the peat moss to 3 gallons)

Even gardeners in cold-winter regions can grow frost-tender dwarf citrus if they garden in containers and overwinter trees indoors.

Strawberries require a sandy, humusy mix:

1 gallon milled peat moss

1 gallon composted manure

1 gallon compost

1 gallon ground fir or pine bark

2 gallons sharp builder's sand

Blending bulk materials is easy to do on a large (9′ × 12′) vinyl tarp. Spread the tarp on a flat surface and start with a cone of topsoil or compost. Spritz the topsoil lightly to keep down the dust and make a dent in the top of the pile. Add the amendments a gallon or two at a time. Pull up the mix from the bottom of the cone and turn over the pile several times with a spade until everything is thoroughly mixed. Store leftover mix in clean 33-gallon garbage cans or bags.

USING FERTILIZERS—
ORGANIC VS. CHEMICAL

Before chemists became involved in agriculture, farmers and gardeners used natural fertilizers such as barnyard and pasture manures and organic wastes. Yields were modest, but the flavor of crops produced by the time-honored methods was far superior to that of produce grown today.

To help farmers coax more and better harvests from their land, chemical fertilizers were introduced. Amateur and professional growers immediately liked the convenience, the fast response and the bountiful yields the chemicals offered. Soon, just about everyone who worked with the soil was using these "miracle" synthetics.

Synthetic plant foods are, as the name implies, inorganic products. There are dozens of brands on the market available in hundreds of percentage combinations of the three primary nutrients—nitrogen, phosphorous and potash, plus some trace elements. For example, you can buy a 10•10•10 analysis fertilizer, or a 5•10•5, or a 10•5•10 and so on. Farmers can order chemical fertilizers formulated for specific crops—foods with 82% nitrogen (anhydrous ammonia) or 53% potash (muriate of potash).

It has only been in the last generation that the true cost of chemical fertilizers has been tallied. First, they can destroy beneficial microorganisms in the soil and contrib-

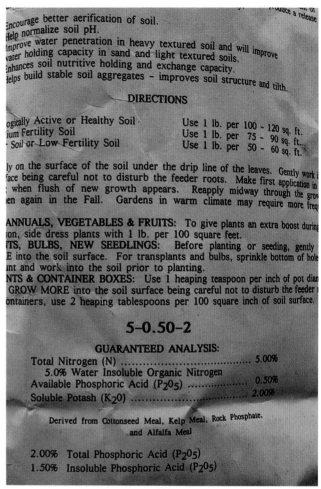

Encourage better aerification of soil.
Help normalize soil pH.
Improve water penetration in heavy textured soil and will improve water holding capacity in sand and light textured soils.
Enhances soil nutritive holding and exchange capacity.
Helps build stable soil aggregates - improves soil structure and tilth.

DIRECTIONS

...ogically Active or Healthy Soil — Use 1 lb. per 100 - 120 sq. ft.
...ium Fertility Soil — Use 1 lb. per 75 - 90 sq. ft.
- Soil or Low Fertility Soil — Use 1 lb. per 50 - 60 sq. ft.

...ly on the surface of the soil under the drip line of the leaves. Gently work ...face being careful not to disturb the feeder roots. Make first application in ... when flush of new growth appears. Reapply midway through the gro... ...en again in the Fall. Gardens in warm climate may require more freq...

ANNUALS, VEGETABLES & FRUITS: To give plants an extra boost durin...
...son, side dress plants with 1 lb. per 100 square feet.
...TS, BULBS, NEW SEEDLINGS: Before planting or seeding, gently ...E into the soil surface. For transplants and bulbs, sprinkle bottom of hole...
...nt and work into the soil prior to planting.
...NTS & CONTAINER BOXES: Use 1 heaping teaspoon per inch of pot diam... ...GROW MORE into the soil surface being careful not to disturb the feeder ...ontainers, use 2 heaping tablespoons per 100 square inch of soil surface.

5-0.50-2
GUARANTEED ANALYSIS:

Total Nitrogen (N) 5.00%
  5.0% Water Insoluble Organic Nitrogen
Available Phosphoric Acid (P_2O_5) 0.50%
Soluble Potash (K_2O) 2.00%

Derived from Cottonseed Meal, Kelp Meal, Rock Phosphate, and Alfalfa Meal

2.00% Total Phosphoric Acid (P_2O_5)
1.50% Insoluble Phosphoric Acid (P_2O_5)

Fertilizer labels reveal exactly what is in the container, including trace elements of important nutrients.

ute to the deterioration of soil friability. Because they dissolve easily in water, they percolate down into the soil where they pollute ground water. Runoff of water containing chemical fertilizer residue from farmlands and large gardens contaminates rivers and streams and can kill off aquatic life.

Eventually, the use of synthesized fertilizers can make the ground where they are used so saturated with acids and salts that the structure of the soil is changed and nothing more can be grown in it. Some farmers in Iowa and vintners in California saw this happening to their soil years ago and turned to organics to restore its vitality and balance.

Time-release organic fertilizers dissolve over several weeks as plants are irrigated, giving steady, gentle nutrition.

Today, the productivity of these farms and vineyards is comparable to what it was before when chemicals were heavily used. The difference is that the rebuilt soil will continue to nourish crops for decades to come while many hundreds of thousands of acres that have been laced with synthetic fertilizers for years will eventually become barren, along with the rivers and streams their runoff has polluted.

Organic Fertilizers

With the growing awareness of the benefits of natural products, many gardeners are turning away from chemical-based or synthesized fertilizers (and pesticides) and are embracing organic forms.

Organic usually means one thing to a gardener and something else to a maker of synthetic fertilizers. To the average person, natural and organic are synonymous with purity—something free of man-made chemicals. Some chemical companies define organic as being a carbon-based element, so this entitles them to label their synthesized nitrogen fertilizers organic, or "natural."

Organic fertilizers are generally low in nitrogen—even dried blood has only a 10% nitrogen content—and break down slowly in the soil. This form of nitrogen is called slow-release or water-insoluble and is transformed by soil microorganisms into a form they can use. On a fertilizer package, water-insoluble nitrogen is often listed as WIN. The higher the WIN percentage, the more slowly the nitrogen is broken down and absorbed. So, the WIN listing is a fairly foolproof way of separating the organics from the chemicals.

Unlike chemical fertilizers, organics add humus and structure to the soil as they decompose. Over the years, soil that has been conditioned by organic amendments becomes so well balanced and nutrient-rich, little, if any, fertilizer is needed to raise healthy plants and productive crops.

Compared with chemical foods that are produced by the ton each month, organics take longer to prepare. Consequently, the cost of chemical fertilizers is about half what a comparable amount of organic food retails for. But the benefits of organics are considered by many gardeners to be worth the added cost. One of these benefits is that organics nourish plants over a long period while chemicals have a green-up effect that, although quick in response, is short-lived nutrition.

Some organics are called "incomplete fertilizers," which means they may be lacking in one or two of the major nutritive elements, nitrogen, phosphorous, or potassium. Blood meal, which has no potassium, is an incomplete fertilizer. Organics with only one of the three elements are called "single fertilizers" and are used to correct a specific nutritional deficiency in a plant. Bone meal is considered a single fertilizer because it is primarily phosphorous-based, with only a trace of nitrogen and potassium.

Organic fertilizers that are commonly available include alfalfa meal, barnyard (poultry) manure, bat guano, blood

A variety of plants, shrubs, and trees in containers are used here to create a front-entry privacy screen.

meal, bone meal, cottonseed meal, kelp/seaweed meal, soybean meal, and steer manure.

Study the analysis of each organic (usually printed on the package), to determine which one is best for nourishing the types of plants you'll be growing.

What Fertilizers Do for Garden Plants

Few gardeners are fortunate enough to have fertile loam that is properly balanced with all the elements that contribute to growth—nitrogen, phosphorous, potassium and trace elements which include boron, copper, iron, magnesium, manganese, molybdenum, sulfur, and zinc.

To understand the importance of the major elements, one must grasp what they contribute to plant nutrition and health. First, nitrogen is one of the most useful of all the

elements. It is essential for good leaf development and color and is crucial in the culture of foliage ornamentals and crop plants. Too much nitrogen, however, weakens plants and, in flowering plants and fruiting crops, an excess can hinder the formation of buds and fruit.

Organic sources of nitrogen are compost, barnyard and pasture manures, cottonseed meal, and dried blood.

Although all the benefits of phosphorous are not known, what is known is that it contributes to healthy growth and seed development and viability. Studies have shown that it helps crop plants produce better and mature sooner, boosts the vitamin content of crops, and infuses plants with greater disease resistance.

Good organic sources of phosphorous include phosphate rock, bone meal, cottonseed meal, and dried blood. Of these, phosphate rock is probably the best source of phosphorous for the gardener. In addition to its high phosphorous content that is broken down quickly in the soil, it also contains a number of beneficial trace minerals. It is most effective when used in combination with manures that are added first, then followed 2–3 weeks later with the ground phosphate.

Potassium, or potash, spurs fast growth of seedlings and helps produce strong stems and vigorous root development. With vegetables and fruit, it contributes to the development of the natural color and flavor of both. A deficiency of potassium leads to poor yields in crop plants and foliage that has browned-off edges or dead areas on leaf surfaces in ornamentals.

There are several sources of naturally produced potassium. Among these are granite dust, greensand (also called glauconite potash), seaweed, and wood ashes.

Although you can blend your own organic fertilizers, it is often more convenient to buy them already mixed with information on how and when to use them printed on the package.

Using Mulches

Organic and inorganic mulches are of great value in retaining soil moisture so that less water is lost through evaporation, in keeping the soil warm, which benefits seedlings planted in early spring before the arrival of seasonal heat,

Nicely staged pots of color and climbers help "landscape" an otherwise barren deck.

This handsome planter is used as a divider between two detached townhouses to delineate property boundaries.

A series of attractively designed planters serves double duty as retaining walls along this driveway.

and in denying weed seeds access to the light they need to germinate.

Organic mulches have been favored by gardeners as long as there have been gardens. These natural (made by nature) materials include weed-free straw, leaf mold, compost, salt marsh hay, pine needles, shredded or ground bark, lawn clippings, animal manures mixed with straw or other oganic material, apple and grape pomace, sawdust, gravel, stones, and a number of products gleaned from harvesting crops, such as peanut hulls. An additional benefit of organic mulches (with the exception of gravel and stones) is that most break down in the earth and, as they mix with the soil, improve its tilth and fertility.

Inorganic mulches are usually easier to handle, more readily found, and considerably cheaper. These include black and clear polyethylene (available in rolls of various widths and lengths), newspapers, so-called landscape fabrics made of vinyl, and other flexible materials (some of which decompose after a few months), and aluminum foil.

Black plastic is a popular mulching material because its opaqueness blocks the germination of weeds. It also warms the soil slightly and helps retain soil moisture. Clear plastic film heats the soil even more because short light rays can pass through it. This may also promote some weed germination, but this is usually minimal. Its primary benefit is warming the soil in early spring and hastening

Cacti and other succulents are ideal low-maintenance plants for balconies, terraces, and sunny windows.

With no space to garden below, this homeowner turned his rooftop into a productive vegetable garden.

the maturity of vegetable crops. Typically, slits in the shape of a cross are made in plastic mulches and seedlings are inserted through these openings and into the soil beneath.

With the arrival of warm weather, plastic mulches are usually removed, but some gardeners leave them in place year round, renewing them periodically and covering them with an organic mulch for appearance and to preserve them against the deteriorating effects of UV rays.

Newspapers are effective as a mulching material, although their appearance may leave something to be desired. They eventually degrade if left in place.

Like plastic mulches, aluminum foil keeps weeds in check and has a warming effect on the soil. An added benefit is that foil reflects light onto the undersides of leaves and this discourages aphids, which establish colonies on foliage out of the sunlight.

c h a p t e r

6

Planting & Care of Contained Gardens

This stunning container garden near the entry dazzles arriving guests. Owners change plants with the seasons.

Above-ground gardens, especially those in portable containers and planters, may be established weeks earlier than it is possible to start a conventional garden in cold-winter regions. This is because the frost and moisture in the ground must be gone before the soil can be worked or plants and seeds will quickly deteriorate in the cold muck.

Even though the air temperature may still be cool, and there may be a chance of a lingering frost, plants and seeds may be started in these areas in movable containers that are filled with custom soilless mixes. If a frost is forecast,

(Page 106) Greenery in planters is used to soften the impact of extensive brick paving.

(Previous page) Staged planters create a stunning effect.

portable planters may be moved under a portective overhang or covered with plastic or fabric attached to stakes. This will create a protective canopy over seedlings, sheltering them from the frigid air.

If you live in a temperate region, generally zones 9 and 10, gardening may be a year-round activity, and you can set up above-ground gardens in either the spring or fall. This is a definite advantage if you are growing vegetables. You can set in the cool-season cole crops and other plants that thrive in the extra moisture and mildness the winter season brings to the Sunbelt.

PLANTING SHRUBS AND TREES

Most trees, shrubs and some bramble berries are offered for sale either in a container or bare root. Some nurseries also package trees and shrubs as balled-and-burlapped specimens (B&Bs), which are similar to bare roots. Both B&Bs and bare roots are harvested from growing fields and greenhouses. The soil is removed from the roots of bare roots (hence, the name) and they are packed in sawdust, peat moss, wood shavings, or other moisture-holding material, then wrapped usually in plastic, to keep the roots moist and viable while they travel to market.

B&Bs are prepared in a similar fashion. They are dug with a soil ball around their roots that will insulate and nourish the plant while it is in transit and during storage. Burlap is wrapped around the roots and tied in place with study twine.

None of these methods is better than another, although bare roots are often less expensive than pot-grown and B&B specimens and they seem to adapt faster. This may be because bare roots are dormant when planted, while those of plants in containers are actively growing and may go into temporary shock when they are disturbed by removing the plant from its can.

Moderately pot-bound trees and shrubs should have their roots loosened and uncoiled before being repotted or planted.

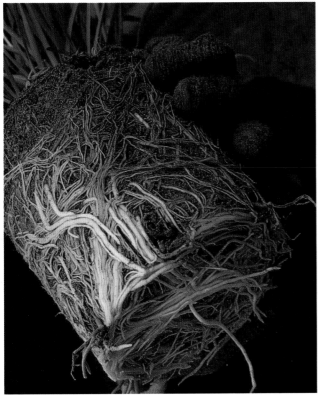

Plants as severely pot-bound as this may be difficult to save. Check plants annually to see if they need moving up to larger containers.

This shock usually is aggravated by the fact that container-grown shrubs and trees often are mildly to seriously pot-bound when you buy them, which means their roots have coiled around each other inside the can and may be growing out the drainage holes. This occurs when inventory doesn't move quickly through the nursery and stock is held for two and even three seasons before it sells.

Pot-bound plants, especially trees, are not the ideal candidates for one's garden. If the roots have been cramped too long, they may have deteriorated to the point where the tree may never realize its original potential. But, if roots can be loosened by pulling or prying them free, the plant should recover. Even so, it's sometimes a good idea to score the root ball with a mat knife in four or five places by making vertical slices with the blade. New roots will develop from the cut areas after planting.

Set the plant into the bed, planter, or container slightly (1–2″) higher than it was growing at the nursery. You can determine the growing height of shrubs and trees by finding the point on the stem or trunk where light bark meets dark bark. Darkly discolored bark indicates the portion of the trunk that was below ground. So, when you set the plant into its new planting hole, position it an inch or two higher than soil level. This is done by placing a stake across the hole and gauging the proper height against the stake. As the tree is watered over the next few weeks, the loosely packed soil mix under it will sink down and the tree will settle to its correct planting depth.

With B&Bs, the burlap does not have to be removed before planting the shrub or tree. Set the plant in place, loosen the ties holding the burlap around the trunk and fold it back. It will rot away in the ensuing months.

To plant bare roots, first remove the insulating material carefully from around the root ball. Examine the roots for

Shrubs and trees are planted 1–2" higher than they were growing in the nursery container. After a few months, they settle to grade level.

When establishing a garden, opt for seedling plants. They adapt faster and with fewer problems, although admittedly larger plants are more impressive.

damage. Any that are broken, discolored (indicating decay) or too long to fit into the container or planter should be snipped off with sharp secateurs. Dull blades crush tissue and this can open the roots to invasion by disease pathogens.

Once the roots have been trimmed (if necessary), plunge them in a bucket of tepid, muddy water and let them soak overnight. This will replace some of the moisture lost since the plant was uprooted. The mud will coat the roots and seal them against any further dehydration.

To plant container-grown and B&B specimens, set the plant in the prepared hole, making sure it is at the proper height, and begin shoveling in planting mix. Tamp the mix down firmly as you go with the heel of your hand. When the hole is half-filled, irrigate and wait for the water to drain away. Then, continue to fill the hole around the roots without tamping until you've reached the proper level.

Bare roots are correctly planted by preparing a mound of soil in the bottom of the hole or container high enough so that when the roots are spread over it, the crown where the dark bark meets light is an inch above the finished soil level. Hold the trunk upright and centered as you scoop in mix around the splayed roots. Firm the mix as before and, when the hole is half-filled, irrigate and finish planting.

Bare roots usually need to be staked until they develop a vigorous root system that stabilizes the plant in its new location. Loosely tie gardener's plastic ribbon around the

trunk and lash it to a stake driven 6″–8″ from the trunk. After the first growing season, the stake may be removed, if desired, since the specimen should be firmly anchored in place after a few months.

Heavy pruning of newly planted shrubs and trees is not necessary and may be detrimental to the health of the plant. Studies in recent years have revealed that shrubs and trees need the foliage that was previously pruned off for photosynthesis (food-making). The only pruning that is recommended is to snip growing tips (except on coniferous plants), and to remove branches that are injured or detract from the shape and proper branch structure.

If you are using soilless mixes, before planting or seed-

Bare root planting calls for building a mound of soil in the planting hole the roots are spread over.

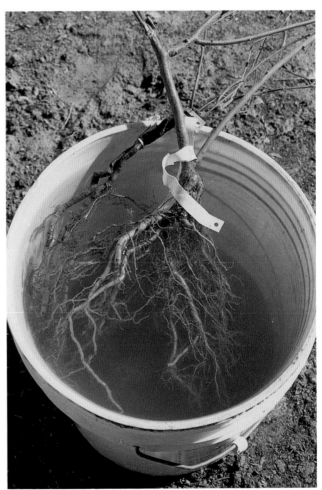

Before planting, soak bare roots in a bucket of muddy water to replenish moisture lost in transit and storage.

Planting & Care of Contained Gardens

Seedling trees and bare roots should be staked for the first season to prevent uprooting by harsh winds.

More mature trees may be trained to grow upright by lashing them to a stake on opposing sides with padded ties.

ing, first wet them down over a day or two to compact them. You may discover that more mix is needed to fill the bed or planter to the desired height once the particles have settled.

PRUNING AND THINNING

There are two kinds of pruning—"therapeutic," in which branches and stems are removed to correct a problem, and "enhancement," in which cuts are made to promote more abundant floral or foliage development, to preserve the natural shape and beauty of a shrub or tree, or to produce a special effect, such as topiary or espaliering.

It is extremely important that you prune shrubs and trees at the right time of year to avoid creating problems, such as removing flowering wood too early or encouraging tender new growth too late in the season only to see it killed by ensuing freezes. Follow this schedule as a general rule of thumb, bearing in mind there are exceptions:

TYPE	WHEN TO PRUNE
Deciduous shrubs and trees that bloom before mid-May.	*When blooms have faded.*

FOR BLOOMS: This type blooms on old (last year's) wood. Cut back stems or branches after flowering to a branch axis

Eastern redbud (Cercis canadensis)

*Evergreen pear (*Pyrus kawakamii*)*

Pruning cuts should be made with clean, sharp secateurs or loppers. Branches removed next to the trunk must be cut off straight and as close to the trunk as possible without injuring the bark. A callus will form over the cut, sealing the injury. Don't leave a stub. Stubs usually die back to the trunk and can take the growth above the cut with them.

Pruning cuts are made at about a 45° angle ⅛″–¼″ above a dormant bud. (See illustration.) You don't have to coat the cut with pruning wound sealer. This was once thought to protect trees against infection and insect invasion, but has since been found to hamper the callusing process.

Trees or shrubs that begin to grow too tall for their tub or box should not topped. When the leader, or main trunk,

(where the stem joins the branch).

FOR CORRECTIVE PURPOSES: Take out crossing branches and all diseased or dead wood. Remove suckers and water sprouts at their source. Head back branch tips to control height and encourage fullness.

Deciduous shrubs and   **January 1 to March 1**
trees that bloom after
mid-May.

FOR BLOOMS: These bloom on new wood (current season's growth). Head back old wood to a branch axis.
FOR CORRECTIVE PURPOSES: (See above and follow the same process.)

Broadleaf evergreen   **Early May**
trees and shrubs.

FOR CORRECTIVE PURPOSES: Same as for deciduous shrubs, trees. Prune to rejuvenate shrubs and trees that lack vigor. Cutting back growing tips will force new growth lower down on branches. Take out some inside branches to admit light to the interior of shrub or tree.

Conifers.   **Late fall**

FOR CORRECTIVE PURPOSES: Prune only to take out diseased or dead wood or to open up shrub or tree. Do not nip back tips unless training yews and similar species as hedges.

Pruning should be done using sharp secateurs with cuts that leave a stub no longer than about 1/8″.

45° ——————————— ⅛″–¼″

Pruning cuts are always made at a 45° angle.

is cut back, the natural shape of the trees is destroyed and the tree compensates for the loss of its leader by putting out a number of what are called epicormic shoots.

Branches may, however, be tipped by taking them back three or four inches to keep a tree or shrub shorter and fuller. A contained tree that is reaching for new heights may have to be transplanted into the garden.

WINTER CARE FOR SHRUBS AND TREES

Most shrubs and trees are dormant during winter, rebuilding their energy for next year's foliage, flowers, and fruit. Even in mild-winter areas, where gardening is an all-year avocation, growth slows to a snail's pace until the arrival of spring weather.

If you live in a region where winters are severe, some of the ornamentals in your above-ground (as well as your conventional) garden may need a little help withstanding the rigors of winter's biting winds and frigid temperatures.

Shallow-rooted plants like azaleas can be damaged by heaving, which is caused by repeated freezing and thawing. After the first ground freeze, mound up insulating material over the plant's crown. Use compost, straw, pine boughs, or ground bark for insulation and cover this with soil several inches deep to keep strong winds from blowing lighter weight mulching material away. In areas with harsh winters, roses especially need protection, particularly the graft union—the point where the rose variety was grafted onto the rootstock.

Where cutting winter winds are prevalent, install windbreaks around broadleaf and needleleaf evergreen varieties, especially if they have suffered previous wind damage. Exposed rhododendrons are, perhaps, the most

*Eley crab apple (*Malus purpurea *'Eleyi')*

vulnerable; strong, frigid winds can shred their foliage, snap branches, and draw moisture out of the leaves that can't be replaced because the sap is frozen.

To protect shrubs such as boxwood, yew, and juniper from breaking under heavy snow loads, wrap them with chicken wire. Snow damage is most likely to befall shrubs growing under roof eaves, where ice and snow sliding off the roof can come crashing down.

Winter wind and sun can dry out needles and leaves, and when the ground is frozen, the roots can't absorb and disperse water to replace the lost moisture. Applying an anti-dessicant spray will help evergreens retain moisture. These sprays may also be used to keep needles on both cut

Built-in planters around pools help soften the impact of a mass of paving. This planting will eventually provide some privacy for the spa.

*Evergreen pear (***Pyrus kawakamii***)*

and live Christmas trees from drying out while they are indoors.

Young fall-planted saplings, fruit trees and others with thin bark also need extra protection. Young trees in areas where seasonal winds are strong and destructive should be staked at planting time because their rudimentary root system has not developed sufficiently to anchor them against strong winds.

The smooth bark of maples and fruit trees tends to split from sunscald, which results from the bark being warmed by the daytime sun and chilled rapidly during plummeting nighttime temperatures. Splits not only worsen through the winter, they also open the door to disease and insect invasions next spring. Protect smooth-bark tree trunks with tree wraps or a coating of white latex (water-base) paint.

Deer, rabbits, and other pests that gnaw at tender trunks can weaken and even kill young trees by girdling the bark. This can be prevented by wrapping the trunks with chicken wire or ¼″ hardware cloth, or by using rigid plastic trunk protectors stocked by many garden centers. These should extend at least 2′ above snow level.

Use sturdy cord or rope to lash together loose, flexible branches of evergreens that might break from snowloads or wind-whipping. This is especially important for shrubs planted near the foundation. Shrubs and trees in planters under eaves are often bombarded by avalanches of snow tumbling off the roof. Periodically shake or knock snow buildup off evergreens to prevent drooping and branch breakage.

Water trees and shrubs up to the first freeze and during any winter thaws. While deciduous trees can usually survive without additional water until spring, evergreens transpire more by passing water vapor to the atmosphere through their pores. Without the extra water, the wind and cold of winter can cause dehydration of leaves and needles, giving them a singed or burned appearance.

With roses, old fashioned varieties are the most winter-hardy. Hybrid teas, floribundas, and grandifloras are the least cold resistant. Roses need protection in areas where temperatures routinely drop below zero in winter. As with trees, it is important to prevent damage caused by heaving which, as mentioned earlier, is caused by cycles of freezing

An attractive row of containerized trees and under-planting of blooming material makes a dramatic statement.

followed by thawing during mutable winter weather. If temperatures seldom drop below zero, you can protect roses by building an 8″ mound of soil, compost, or other mulch around the crown of each plant. In colder regions, build a 12″-thick mound and cover it with a loose mulch of pine boughs, oak leaves, or straw held in place with mesh or weighted-down chicken wire. In areas where temperatures plummet to −15°F or lower and remain there for long periods, completely enclose rose shrubs with caps, cones, baskets and other covers.

To protect less hardy roses in all cold-winter regions, strip foliage from shrubs, water them well and apply a fungicide just before the first hard freeze is due. Prune branches to half their original height and lash canes se-

*Azalea (*Rhododendron *sp.)*

*Saucer magnolia (*Magnolia soulangiana*)*

curely together with twine. Add mounding material at the base and once the ground freezes, cover the mounds with loose mulch.

Hygiene in the garden is important, especially at the end of the growing season. Clean up fallen fruit and other debris that might provide a haven in which insects can overwinter and thrive the following spring. Remove and destroy bagworm cases and egg masses as well as any gypsy moth or tent caterpillar colonies found around the garden. Gypsy moth egg cases look like smudges of peanut butter. If you don't get rid of the egg cases, hoards of hungry caterpillars will strip foliage from the host tree the following spring and summer.

DEALING WITH PESTS AND DISEASES

For nearly every destructive pest or disease encountered in the garden, there is an organic prevention or control. No longer is it necessary to resort to lethal chemicals and synthetics that contain dangerous ingredients and leave harmful, long-lived residues behind. A number of new organics have been introduced in the last few years that are effective against a host of sucking and chewing insects and devitalizing diseases.

While most chemical pesticides are non-selective, broad-spectrum killers that wipe out most insects with which they come in contact, including beneficials like honeybees and lady beetles, organics are selective, which means they target one or two specific pests or problems. Chemicals have a quick "knock down" of pests and a long residual kill potential. Organics usually take time since many of them work by disrupting the digestive system of insects, and they have a short life.

Residues of chemical pesticides create a problem for the environment when runoff from water containing these deadly concoctions filters down into aquifers containing ground water reservoirs or migrates into streams and rivers where fish and other marine life are threatened.

This may sound like an extreme scenario. A fair question to ask is: How can one gardener using a chemical pesticide affect the environment? The answer is that the one gardener's use must be multiplied several millionfold to include all the home gardeners who may be using "just a little" pesticide. Each year, home gardeners in the U.S. use over *300 million pounds* of chemical pesticides. Add this to the 2.7 billion pounds sprayed and dusted annually on commercially grown crops and the severity of the situation becomes clear.

What is not commonly known, except to farmers and makers of chemical pesticides, is that insects are constantly building up resistance to the chemicals that once could kill them on contact. They mutate into superbugs for which we have no sprays or dusts. The chemical companies continually respond by making deadlier and more persistant pesticides in what may soon become an apocalyptic game of one-upsmanship, a game mankind cannot win.

It may not be too great a stretch of the imagination to wonder if the cause of the rare types of cancer that have sprung up in the last decade might not be traced some day to an overuse of man-made chemical pesticides on the nation's produce.

These chemical timebombs aren't necessary to control pests in the garden or in commercial farming operations, for that matter. While organics may work a bit more slowly and may need to be repeated to eliminate the problem, they *do* work and do so without imperiling the environment.

Most informed and responsible gardeners have adopted an integrated pest management (IPM) program to deal with pests. This strategy involves a combination of controls that include hand picking of damaging insects, using a variety of traps to snare harmful pests, and setting natural

Lady beetles feasting on aphids. Aphids devitalize a host of plants by sucking out life-sustaining sap.

Planting & Care of Contained Gardens
119

predators against pests to reduce or eliminate their populations. As a last resort, organic pesticides are used when other measures prove to be ineffective.

When using any pesticide, follow the user directions faithfully. Resist the urge to embrace the myth that if a little is good, a lot is better. First, try the product at the time and strength and using the procedure recommended on the package. If results are unsatisfactory, explore other solutions. A second application may do the trick, or another organic may be more effective.

One of the tenets of IPM gardening is to seek out pest- and disease-resistant varieties of the plant you want to grow. All those millions of dollars in R&D investment by seedsmen, the USDA and agricultural colleges has produced a wide choice of cultivars for many popular home garden ornamentals and crop plants.

Tomatoes are a prime example. While heirlooms that your grandfather may have grown back on the old homestead are making a strong comeback because of their marvelous flavor or interesting color, these open-pollinated varieties are often struck down by verticillium or fusarium wilts (although some may have built up a resistance to one or both diseases). Today's crop of hybrid tomatoes may not have the distinctive flavor of their old fashioned ancestors, but they do have bred into their genetic makeup a resistance to wilts and nematodes and are labeled VFN hybrids. A few are only resistant to verticillium and fusarium wilts (called VF hybrids), but if nematodes are a problem, they can usually be destroyed organically.

Organic Pesticides

As mentioned earlier, true organic compounds are distilled from natural sources, as opposed to chemicals, which are synthesized in the laboratory. Nothing inorganic is added to enhance the "kill potential" or longevity of organics.

BACILLUS THURINGIENSIS, commonly called B.t. The strain *B. t. kurstaki* (B.t.k.) is used to control borer insects. *B.t.* 'San Diego' controls Colorado potato beetles and elm leaf beetles. This microbial insecticide is commonly available as a wettable powder and may be found in liquid form. It works by paralyzing the digestive system of insects.

AZADIRACHTIN, or **NEEM,** is a botanical extract taken from the seeds of the margosa tree *(Azadirachta indica)*. It is effective against such sucking insects as aphids, leafminers, thrips and whiteflies in the juvenile stage of development. Like B.t., it is a feeding inhibitor that interrupts the digestive process of pests feeding on it.

DIATOMACEOUS EARTH, popularly called D.E., is not technically a pesticide, but it is an organic compound that is effective against soft-bodied pests like aphids, caterpillars, leafhoppers, slugs, snails and sowbugs. It is composed of abrasive silica shells that are like tiny slivers of razor blades. These are called diatoms, and they can easily pene-

Insecticidal soap is effective as a safe insecticide against aphids, whiteflies, and a number of other soft-bodied pests.

trate an insect's body, causing it to, in a sense, bleed to death through the wounds inflicted by the diatoms. There is evidence that D.E. also kills earthworms, so use it only where none are present, if you want to preserve these valuable creatures.

INSECTICIDAL SOAP is made from fatty acids produced by plants and animals. There are different formulations for use on specific plants. It acts as a contact poison on soft-bodied pests such as aphids, caterpillars, mealybugs, slugs, snails, thrips, and whiteflies. These soaps may be effective against some hard-bodied pests (scales, etc.) in their immature stages. They kill on contact by penetrating the insect's body and destroying membranes. Best used in the morning and evening.

NICOTINE SULFATE is a deadly alkaloid extracted from tobacco plants. Available as a dust or liquid, it is extremely toxic to humans and animals and printed instructions and precautions should be followed to the letter. It is a non-selective contact poison effective against a broad range of sucking insects. Used only as a last resort because of its toxicity.

HORTICULTURAL OILS, also called dormant and summer oils. For decades, horitcultural oils were used as dormant sprays on deciduous plants in fall and winter because they were too heavy and impure to use on foliage. Today's new generation of horticultural oils are lighter and purer. Popularly called summer, superior, or supreme oils, they work by covering insects and their eggs with an impermeable layer of oil that smothers them. The newer oils may be used as a dormant spray to control overwintering pests and as a summer spray to eradicate new invasions. Follow label directions and cautions against use on species that may be damaged by oils.

PYRETHRIN, also called Pyrethrum, is a broad spectrum botanical made from the flowers of *Chrysanthemum cinerariifolium (C. cinerariaefolium)*. It is available in liquid and dust forms and is sometimes combined with other natural insecticides or fungicides for faster or more sustained control or for dealing with two problems at once. It is a nerve poison that is effective against a wide spectrum of chewing and sucking pests. It is lethal to lady beetles and may be toxic to certain mammals.

Both pyrethrin and rotenone organic pesticides come in dust form for sprinkling on food crops. They have a short effective life.

ROTENONE, often called derris, is derived primarily from derris and cube barbasco, two tropical plants. It is both a stomach and contact poison that is often diluted with pyrethrin and ryania because of its potency. It is highly effective against caterpillars and Japanese beetles and is available as a dust, wettable powder, or liquid concentrate.

RYANIA is made from the South American shrub *Ryania speciosa* and is a powerful botanical that is effective against a host of chewing and sucking pests, including aphids, coddling moth larvae, European corn borers, Japanese beetles, and thrips. It is toxic to aquatic life.

To control tomato hornworms organically, dust plants with Bacillus thuringiensis *(B.t.), an effective control.*

SABADILLA A popular Old World pesticide made from the South American plant *Schoenocaulon officinale*. It is an effective stomach poison against many garden pests including aphids, blister beetles, caterpillars, grasshoppers, leafhoppers, squash bugs, stink bugs, and thrips. It is lethal to honeybees, but rated harmless to other beneficials.

Other Organic Solutions

In addition to the foregoing, there are other organics that are effective alternatives to chemicals. One of the oldest weapons in the gardener's arsenal is **garlic oil spray**. It can easily be made by finely chopping six large, fresh garlic cloves and adding a tablespoon of mineral oil. Allow this to steep overnight, then add a tablespoon of pure liquid soap (containing no scents or dyes) and two cups of warm water. Mix thoroughly with a spoon, then strain off the concentrate into a storage container. To use, add two tablespoons of concentrate to one pint of warm water and pour into a hand misting bottle.

STICKY BARRIERS are made by using a tacky substance, sold under a variety of trade names such as Tanglefoot, which is composed of castor oil, natural gum resins, and vegetable waxes. Bands of cardboard are taped around plant stems or tree trunks near the soil line and the sticky

Tacky barriers such as "Tanglefoot" spread in a band around tree trunks trap crawling insect pests.

Sticky yellow insect traps attract several types of flying pests, especially whiteflies.

goo is spread around the cardboard ring with a knife or spatula. Insects that try to pass through the barrier become trapped.

STICKY BOARDS are similar in concept. These are sheets of durable cardboard impregnated with wax tinted white or yellow (the colors that attract a number of flying garden pests) and coated with a sticky resin. These are attached to stakes that are placed in the garden. They are especially effective against whiteflies and fungus gnats.

PHEROMONE TRAPS The mating urge is a strong one, even in the insect world. Science has synthesized the scent emitted by a variety of female pests when they are ready to mate. This scent, when affixed to a trap, lures hopeful males of the species to their death. The sex-bait trap for attracting Japanese beetles is extremely effective. Baits are available for controlling other pests, including apple maggots and apple sawflies.

Precautions When Using Organics

Organic pesticides, like organic fertilizers, are environmentally safe—if used wisely. There are some organics that are toxic to marine and animal life and harmful to humans. Nicotine sulfate is probably the most dangerous, and products containing it usually carry a poison caution. Rotenone, which is made from the roots of certain legumes, is quite toxic to fish and pigs, but is safe to use on crop plants since it leaves no harmful residue.

Use the same precautions and common sense when applying organics as you would when using any potentially harmful chemical. This includes wearing gloves, eye protection, and a respirator as recommended on the product packaging when mixing and applying the solution. Many organics can irritate eye tissue and mucous membranes in the nose and mouth.

Most fungus disease is spread by damp conditions in the garden. Wait for foliage to dry before working around plants.

ORGANIC CONTROLS FOR DISEASES

COMMON NAME	TYPE	TARGETS	PREVENTION	CONTROL
DISEASE/PATHOGEN				
Anthracnose	Fungal	*Cornus, Acer, Plantanus* and other species; Beans, cucumbers, melons, peppers, tomatoes.	Buy resistant varieties. Don't handle wet foliage. Plant in well-drained media. Spray copper-based fungicide.	No effective control once infection occurs. Discard diseased plants.
Bacterial Spot	Bacterial	Pepper, tomatoes and many others.	Proper garden sanitation. Crop rotation. Buy resistant varieties. Copper-based fungicidal sprays.	Some control possible with copper-based fungicide if disease is caught early. Discard plants with advanced stages.
Black Spot	Fungal	*Rosa* species.	Don't use overhead irrigation. Improve air circulation around shrubs. Spray susceptible plants weekly with sulfur.	Prune out infested portions. Spray a 10% baking soda solution. Spray or dust shrubs with bordeaux mix.
Cedar-Apple Rust	Fungal	*Cedrus,* apple species.	Plant apples only if cedars are five miles away. Buy resistant varieties. Use copper-based fungicides as preventive spray. Don't wet foliage during irrigation.	If infection is caught early, lime-sulfur may be effective. Remove and destroy infected portions of trees.
Downy Mildew	Fungal	Many species of ornamental and crop plants.	Improve air circulation around plants and don't wet foliage during irrigation. Buy resistant varieties.	Remove, destroy infected portions. Apply sprays, dusts of copper-based fungicides.
Early, Late Blight	Fungal	Potatoes, tomatoes.	Buy only certified disease-free seed potatoes and blight-resistant tomato varieties. Keep garden free of plant debris. Use spray of copper-based fungicide to prevent early blight.	Remove, destroy infected plants and potatoes. There is no effective control once disease spreads.
Fire Blight	Bacterial	Apples, *Pyrus,* Quinces, *Rosa* species.	Buy resistant varieties.	Remove infected sections with some healthy tissue. Spray bordeaux mix during dormant season.
Fusarium Wilt	Fungal	Many ornamental and crop species. Some hosts are dahlias, melons, peppers and tomatoes.	Solarize soil where wilt has been prevalent. Buy resistant varieties.	No known cure. Remove and destroy infected plants.
Mosaic	Viral	Many ornamental species.	Buy resistant varieties. Use floating row cover to keep out vectors like aphids.	No known cure. Remove, destroy infected plants.
Powdery Mildew	Fungal	Many ornamental and crop species.	Improve air circulation around plants. Buy resistant varieties.	Both 10% baking soda and lime-sulfur sprays somewhat effective in controlling spread of fungal fruiting spores.
Rust	Fungal	Many ornamentals and brambles.	Improve air circulation by thinning and don't wet foliage when irrigating. Dust with sulfur early to prevent infection.	Infected bramble canes should be destroyed. For other species, dusting with sulfur may control spread.

COMMON NAME	TYPE	TARGETS	PREVENTION	CONTROL
Sooty Mold	Fungal	Many ornamental species.	Control honeydew-excreting insects early to eliminate problem.	Remove honeydew and any insects that produce it.
Verticillium Wilt	Fungal	Many ornamentals and crop plants, especially asters, mums, maples, melons, tomatoes, cherries, peaches.	If available, buy wilt-resistant varieties. Solarize soil where wilt has appeared.	No known cure.

Black spot, a fungal disease, attacks roses. Dust susceptible varieties weekly with sulfur.

Powdery mildew is another common fungus that grows and spreads in damp conditions.

ORGANIC CONTROLS FOR PESTS

COMMON NAME	HOUSE PLANTS	TRAPS	BENEFICIAL INSECTS	BACILLUS THURINGIENSIS STRAINS	INSECTICIDAL SOAP	NICOTINE SULFATE
PESTS						
Aphids	X		Green Lacewings Lady Beetles		X	X
Apple Maggot		X	Parasitic Nematodes			
Armyworm			Trichogramma Wasps	B.T.K.		
Asparagus Beetle	X					
Bagworm		X		B.T.K.		
Cabbage Worm, Imported			Trichogramma Wasps	B.T.K.		
Cabbage Looper			Trichogramma Wasps	B.T.K.		
Carrot Rust Fly			Parasitic Nematodes			
Codling Moth			Trichogramma Wasps	B.T.		
Colorado Potato Beetle				B.T. 'San Diego'		
Corn Earworm			Green Lacewings	B.T.K.		
Cucumber Beetle			Parasitic Nematodes			
Cutworm				B.T.	X	
Elm Bark, Leaf Beetle		X	Braconid Wasps	B.T. 'San Diego'		
Geranium Budworm				B.T.		
Grubs			Parasitic Nematodes			
Gypsy Moth		X	Tachinid Flies	B.T.K.		
Japanese Beetle		X	Parasitic Nematodes			
Leafhopper	X		Green Lacewing Lady Beetle		X	
Leafminer		X				
Mealybug	X		Parasitic Wasps Green Lacewing Lady Beetle		X	

HORTICULTURAL OILS	PYRETHRUM	ROTENONE	RYANIA	SABADILLA	OTHER
	X	X		X	
	X	X		X	
X					
	X	X			
					Hand pick, destroy bags
				X	Floating row cover
	X			X	
					Floating row cover
X				X	Floating row cover
	X	X			Spray Neem Hand pick
				X	Spray Neem
	X	X			Floating row cover
					Use collars around stems
	X				Floating row cover
	X				
		X			Floating row cover Milky disease spore
	X	X		X	
X					Floating row cover Nicotine tea

COMMON NAME	HOUSE PLANTS	TRAPS	BENEFICIAL INSECTS	BACILLUS THURINGIENSIS STRAINS	INSECTICIDAL SOAP	NICOTINE SULFATE
Mexican Bean Beetle			Parasitic Wasps			
Mite, Rust						
Mite, Spider	X		Green Lacewing Predatory Mites			
Pear Psylla					X	
Root-Knot Nematode						
Scale	X		Green Lacewing Lady Beetle Predatory Beetles, Wasps		X	
Slug, Snail		X	Decollate Snails			
Squash Bug		X				
Squash Vine Borer						
Tarnished Plant Bug						
Tent Caterpillars				B.T.K.		
Thrips	X		Green Lacewing Lady Beetle Predatory Mites		X	
Tobacco, Tomato Hornworm			Trichogramma Wasps	B.T.K.		
Webworm, Fall			Parasitic Wasps	B.T.K.		
Whitefly	X	X			X	

Common snail, slug

Whiteflies

Aphids

Tent caterpillars

Planters, Containers & Raised Beds

HORTICULTURAL OILS	PYRETHRUM	ROTENONE	RYANIA	SABADILLA	OTHER
	X	X		X	Floating row cover Spray Neem
X					Lime-Sulfur
X					Lime-Sulfur, Sulfur
X					Solarize soil
X					Scale parasites
					Insecticidal dusts Diatomaceous earth
	X	X		X	Floating row cover
	X	X			Floating row cover Remove by slitting vines
		X		X	Floating row cover
					Prune, burn infested branches, destroy tents
	X		X	X	Spray Neem
					Hand pick, destroy
					Prune, destroy infested branches
X	X	X			

Cottony cushion scales

Armored scales

Japanese beetles

Mealybugs

Planting & Care of Contained Gardens

Staying Legal/Working with Professionals

An inviting patio enhanced with thriving hanging baskets and pots of color. Nipping out dying blooms keeps plants setting new buds.

STAYING LEGAL

Most communities in the U.S. have building departments or similar entities whose job is to see that residential and commercial construction is designed and built following specific codes and ordinances. Codes and ordinances are put in place to ensure that projects are built following sound construction techniques for the public safety and to preserve the integrity of laws and ordinances governing height, placement, design, material, and other considerations.

(Page 130) Classical formal garden with raised beds, gravel paths.

(Previous page) Used-brick planter designed to blend with house.

In addition to municipal ordinances, a home in a condominium, planned community development, or historic district, may have other covenants and restrictions governing additions and renovations.

Building Permits

Fortunately, projects such as planters, raised beds and retaining walls under 3' high are generally exempt from the permit process, but not always. In condos and planned communities, the CC&Rs (covenants, codes, and restrictions) may preclude *any* projects. The safest course is to check with your local building department and, if your home is governed by homeowner's association rules, to read your CC&Rs to learn what, if anything, you need to do to ensure compliance with existing codes, ordinances, and restrictions.

If you plan to enclose your front yard with a high court-yard wall containing built-in planters and lighting, you will almost certainly need a permit. Even though the proposed project may not conflict with height or set-back restrictions, inspectors will want to see the footings and reinforcing rod placement, as well as the electric wiring. They will want to be sure the wall will be built solidly and won't fall over some day due to poor design and construction techniques. They will want to determine that the wiring for lighting is installed properly (in conduit, grounded, etc.) and is of the correct gauge and type.

Even if a project doesn't require a permit, it may be governed by local zoning ordinances requiring any construction to comply with codes. In fact, the permit process is basically in place to ensure a compliance on the part of homeowners and contractors with the Uniform Building Code from which most construction codes across the country emanated. It is aimed at maintaining minimum building standards.

Raised beds don't have to be complex to be effective.

Variances

A variance is an official permit which allows a project to be built that is in conflict with current codes. It could be a set-back restriction that states construction may not extend beyond a certain point on a residential lot. In many communities, walls that extend farther than the front elevation of the garage are not permitted because they change the appearance or character of the neighborhood.

Sometimes a variance can be obtained from the local zoning board, but they are seldom granted without persuasive testimony as to why the exception should be made. One thing that can be helpful is a written statement from your neighbors saying they have no objection to the proposed project.

If you apply for a variance, it is crucial that you attend the hearing so you can offer additional arguments and be available to respond to questions from the board members. If you don't appear, the assumption may be that the board's decision isn't that important to you.

There are serious consequences if you build a project that requires a permit or variance and you don't have either. The penalty can be a fine several times the cost of the permit and inspection fee. More likely, you will be required to demolish the project, which means you'll be out the cost of materials and any hired labor to erect it.

Built-in planters become part of the home's architecture.

A few containers of color at the entry walk require very little effort, but the results are captivating.

Planters, Containers & Raised Beds

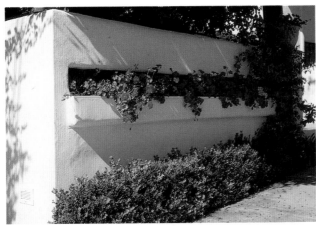

Privacy wall has a cleverly placed niche for plants, which are changed with each season.

WORKING WITH PROFESSIONALS

Knowledgeable do-it-yourselfers know their construction skill limitations and routinely hire a professional to do work that is beyond their level of expertise. As mentioned earlier, there are projects only a licensed expert should tackle, such as designing and constructing retaining walls over 3' tall.

Landscape Designers/Contractors

In nearly every city of moderate size, there are landscape designers and contractors who offer design help and construction services. Both can be found in the yellow pages of your telephone directory, but the best sources are neighbors and friends who are satisfied clients. Building supply companies may also have a list of approved designers or contractors you can consult.

Most landscape designers are also licensed contractors or have aligned themselves with one. In addition to designing gardens and outdoor living features, such as decks, cook-out centers, and raised beds, they also build projects and are popularly called "design-build" firms.

Contractors usually don't design projects, they simply construct them following the plan that is given to them. They buy all the materials, arrange for their delivery to the job site, and hire the workmen who will construct the job.

If you decide to hire a contractor, there are steps you should take to ensure a professional job at the agreed-upon price. While most landscape contractors are honest and reliable, the business is a magnet for bad apples—especially in states like California and Florida where considerable sums are spent on outdoor-living features.

When you hire a contractor, the typical procedure is for you to sign a contract for the work to be performed and materials to be purchased in your behalf. In fact, one should adopt as an iron-clad rule that no work is begun without a signed contract spelling out what work will be performed in a definite time period, how it will be done, who will do it, what special materials, if any, will be used, how much the job will cost, and how payments and disputes will be handled.

It is traditional to pay a deposit of from 10% to 20% of the total cost at the time of contract signing, but this is always negotiable. It is both a good faith payment and an advance to help the contractor pay for materials to get the job underway. Most contracts call for (or should) incremental payments as the work progresses. It is always best to stick to this agreement. Scheduled payments are your "bargaining chips" to ensure that work progresses in a timely and satisfactory manner. If you hand over most of the money up front, you've lost a lot of your leverage with the contractor. One rule that should never be broken is: Never release the final payment until the job has been completed to your satisfaction and all conditions set down in the contract have been met, such as site clean-up and hauling away of debris.

How can you avoid hooking up with one of the fly-by-

Dual planters are the front-yard garden on this small city lot. Such plantings need frequent grooming.

A family vegetable/cutting garden raised out of harm's way from bikes, kids, and dogs.

night operators? By doing what you should always do when hiring craftspeople—first check them out. Most states require contractors to be licensed. Before you sign a contract or hand over any money, ask the contractor for his license number, then call the state contractor licensing board and ask 1) if the license is valid and 2) if the contractor has any complaints or lawsuits lodged against him for dishonest tactics or shoddy workmanship.

Next, ask your potential contractor for at least three client references, then *check them out*. Few homeowners follow through on reference-checking and some live to rue the oversight. In addition to calling the references and asking the appropriate questions, ask if you can come by to look at the project.

It is always smart to work only with licensed contractors. They tend to be more competent, since they must pass a test to receive their license, and more reliable because their license is at stake in many states if too many valid complaints are filed against them with the licensing board. Unlicensed contractors may quote lower fees, but you have no protection against unethical practices or slipshod, incompetent work. Many progressive states require licensed contractors to carry liability insurance to protect you against lawsuits if they, their workmen or visitors are injured on the job site. Unlicensed contractors rarely carry liability insurance.

Once you do hire a contractor, make sure you have a signed contract which specifically spells all the important points described earlier, especially when the job will be started and finished. Some ambitious contractors take on more work than they can handle and are then forced to stretch out jobs or stall clients for weeks or months. This brings up another point—many times busy contractors only put in "special" appearances when they interview for the job, sign the contract, and pick up checks. The rest of the time, you only see their crew. If it is important to you that the contractor be on the site each day or most days to supervise work, this should be clarified in the contract.

If your project is extensive and costly, ask your potential contractor if he would be willing to take out a perfor- mance bond (and give you a copy). This will protect you in the event he fails to complete the job or pay his workmen or subs, and not leave you liable for their compensation, which could be the case. Most reputable contractors are happy to do this.

If you sign a contract, live up to your end regarding payments. Keep in mind that if you don't, many states allow a contractor to put a lien on your home that can prevent its sale, make refinancing difficult or impossible, and some- times even affect your credit rating negatively. Be aware also that change orders after construction has begun can be expensive, especially if construction already installed has to be torn out to accommodate the changes.

This steep hillside site was transformed from a useless part of the landscape into a lovely space by terracing with retaining walls.

Multi-level planters also serve as the walls for the courtyard of this contemporary California home.

Landscape Architects

The elite of landscape designers are the architects who have graduated from a school of landscape architecture, passed a rigorous exam and received a license to practice from the state. Many architects join the American Society of Landscape Architects (ASLA), the professional society that sets the standards for design excellence and ethics for the profession.

Landscape architects are qualified to handle all aspects of design and site-problem solutions, unlike contractors and landscape designers. They are usually more environmentally and aesthetically sensitive. And, they are also the most expensive of the professionals, reflecting their expertise and years of education in the field. Some will consult with you on an hourly rate ($50 and up); others work on a

fee or percentage of the job cost basis. Bear in mind that young architects just getting established are often easier to work with and more concerned with getting practical experience than earning a large fee (an attitude which changes with the acquisition of age and business savvy).

Landscape architects are generally not hired to handle small projects, but are most often retained to design or redesign an entire yard. If you have a problem site, a landscape architect can provide reliable information on how to resolve difficulties and help steer you away from costly mistakes.

Design professionals are knowledgeable about the permit process and what is required for city approval of a proposed project. They can save you time and hassle by preparing the plans and application and pulling the permit for you.

Combination privacy wall/planter/garden-tool- storage structure.

Staying Legal/Working with Professionals

INDEX

Index